The Medusa Trap
Escaping Her Control

THOMAS KATT ESQ.

ISBN -10: 1720451745
ISBN-13: 978-1720451747

DEDICATION

For my grandsons – Josh, Tyler and Eddie

CONTENTS

ACKNOWLEDGMENTS

The experiences of Thomas Katt Esq. provided much of the inspiration for this book, his 'field tests', experiences and openness proving invaluable. Robert Laynton focused these experiences through the lens of psychology theories and wrote the text. Thanks also goes to J.S. for providing invaluable female insight. My appreciation to everyone who provided further anecdotes and/or took part in the lively and fun debates regarding the themes in this book. All illustrations are either 'royalty free' or are originals by Bob Laynton. Front cover photo by Bob Laynton.

1 INTRODUCTION

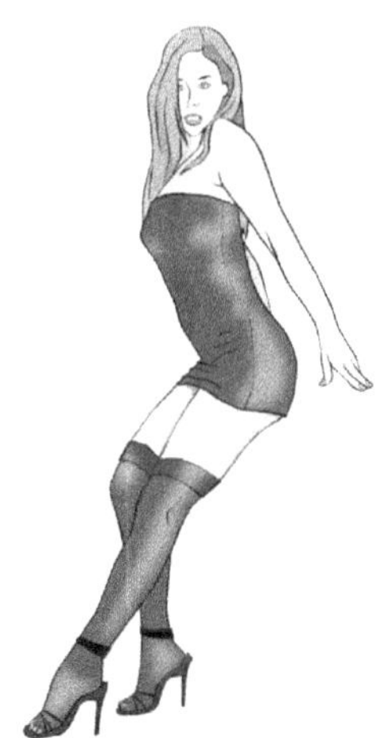

So. Interested in girls huh? Be careful! Girls are a different species, so you will be all the better for help from this book.

Girls are seen as 'experts' in relationships – not good for you - they put stuff in the media from a *girl's* point of view, and have lots of media stuff telling them how to deal with boyfriends like you. But this book takes a *male* point of view. It's on your side and based on successful experience.

Girlfriends want to own you body and soul

Many girls act like mothers. So - surprise, surprise! - their boyfriends act like children. If you are being told off, told what to do, when to do it and how - you won't be right even if you do as you are told. 'Motherly' girlfriends don't like you choosing your own path in life. So if your girlfriend refuses to treat you as someone capable of making your own decisions, then she has to change or you'll walk away.

Here is your first important lesson:

> Your ability to walk away is the greatest power you possess

Differences between males and females cause problems

Males and females are different. **Fact.** But if you say it out loud, girls will put on an authoritative voice and talk about:

Blah Blah. Ignore all that. 'Different' does NOT mean 'unequal', and older ideas are often the best. This book is for *males* – you don't have tits, they don't have a dick.

Trouble is you've been outnumbered from the start - brought up by females even before you went to school. The female view of life was present everywhere in your childhood and it's still there now. In the West, females have eaten away at male values for years. This state of affairs will continue for you if you let your girlfriend act like your mother. She will dismiss things you are interested in and call them 'little boys toys'. She will give you advice and lay down rules whether you ask for them or not. If you let her behave like this, this situation will carry on for the rest of your life.

By behaving like this she oversteps the mark and crosses the boundary line into your private, personal space

Her 'ideal' boyfriend

Girls dream about their 'ideal' boyfriend

Some girlfriends like a rough, roguish boyfriend because they want to 'tame' him.

Some girlfriends say that their boyfriends should be sensitive and caring – washing dishes, vacuuming carpets, cooking meals and so on – a 'good little boy'.

Some girlfriends want a 'Knight in shining armor'......in which case your role will be to show her off at her best and think of her as the glittering prize that you are fighting for and may win – someday, sometime, if she lets you. You will spend the rest of your life opening doors for her, buying her costly presents (she will keep telling you that she's worth it) and seeking to meet her every wish.

Like Sir Walter Raleigh of old, you will keep putting your coat down over muddy puddles so she does not get her dainty little shoes all mussed up.

What you will end up with is mud on your coat AND on your face

But don't end up with an Arnold Schwarzenegger / Dwayne Johnson cartoon-like image of 'maleness' – a two dimensional, muscle-bound, die hard, shoot 'em up, Judge Dredd, Duke Nukem comic-book-superhero version of 'maleness' – that's not the answer.

Pay attention! Her 'ideal' boyfriend will not have his balls cut off in one go – instead, they will be sliced off slice by slice over a long period of time - he will hardly notice it is happening - until it is too late.

Girls want to create their boyfriend in their own image – tame, soft, caring and sensitive - then they will complain that their boyfriend is not very 'manly'

Look at this teenage male who has been brought up by females:

As a boy he was thought of as 'sissy'

As a teenager - shy, awkward and self-conscious

He is well dressed – but hopelessly out of fashion

He has not 'toughened up'

Touching and intimacy make him feel

embarrassed

His sternness, passion and fearlessness have been

undermined

Is it worth it?

Is having a serious relationship with a girl worth the trouble? Yes - as long as you don't walk into their traps. Girls don't prepare you for relationships with girls as an equal partner, companion or  lover – in fact, they hold you back. Girls *talk* about gender equality, but pull the wool over *your* eyes to keep you under control like a 'good little boy' while they keep a 'superior' 'bossy', 'mother-like' role. Your mother won't want you to read this book and girls will tell you that it is 'rubbish' and that it's contents are 'just not true'.

Girls tell you these things so they can stay one up

But when you take responsibility and take charge of yourself, the opportunity will arise for both of you to be happy.

If your girlfriend doesn't make you happy, but drags you down, what's the point?

Using this book

Some of you will read this book, talk about it, try some of its recommendations and then stand on the sidelines to say why these approaches won't work for you – because of your looks, personality, body shape, lifestyle, religious beliefs, past experiences, age, circumstances, colour of your hair, your curly hair, straight hair, lack of hair or whatever. You would be wrong. Successfully relating to girlfriends can be learned – not overnight and you will certainly have some failures - but over time and with practice, you will learn.

If you become a critic you will achieve nothing

If you want to put up with low standards, poor relationships and unhappiness – go ahead - act like a judge. But if you want a decent relationship with the right girl, YOU must put these approaches into PRACTICE - no one will do it for you - certainly not your mother or girlfriend. You need commitment, staying power, dedication - and this book.

Otherwise, put this book down now, go back to your girlfriend and do everything that she tells you for the rest of your life

Puberty

In moving from childhood to adulthood both genders seek to assert themselves as independent young adults. It's not easy. You will find that girls delight, excite, arouse, entertain and give you pleasure and that your feelings and passions will be intense. Extremes will pass but for a while expect:

Pimples

Increased awareness of females

as sexual objects of desire

Being increasingly driven by sexual impulses

– thinking with your cock

Some loss of your cool, cognitive, logical

analytic ability

The female brain undergoes 'rewiring' – new connections are made that result in what you will see as temporary female insanity. Expect:

Emotional upsets - crying,

sulks and tantrums

Dramatic 'flopping' onto the sofa like

a dead weight

Very rapid talking - torrents of words

with lots of 'yea' 'no' 'like' and

'but' words thrown in

A barrage of her roller coaster emotions

All or nothing thinking

Constant criticism and fault-finding:

'What time is it Mom?'

'It's five past three'

'No it isn't, it's SIX minutes past three!'

It's vital that you adopt the view that

Males and females are different

Your girlfriend lives in a different world

If she drags you into her world, you will be hopelessly lost and end up at least one down

Forget fairytale romantic images of females. You don't read fairytales any more so don't be childish. Girls have their dark side.

Girls are:

Snoopers with no guilt about looking at your phone messages

Like snakes with tits

Eager to change you into their image

Eager to trap you in a box of their own making

Eager to pull you into the swamp of emotions

Like a dog with bone - they won't let things go

Loyal to themselves – they will kick you when you are down

Eager to tell you what to do, when to do it and how to do it

QUIZ TIME!

Before you read any further, take some time to answer the
following questions– your answers will help you to
understand how you relate to your girlfriend – and how you
see her relating to you

It will take about 30 minutes. Grab a pen and paper -

Here are two sets of statements - one about how you see yourself, the other about how you see your girlfriend. Look at each statement and rate it with a score between 0 – 5. A score of 0 means you disagree with the statement and 1 - 5 is a scale of increasing agreement - a score of 1 means you slightly agree and a score of 5 means that you totally and absolutely agree.

A quiz about how you see yourself

1) Honesty and straight talking is important to me.

2) I have a very responsible approach to life and relationships.

3) I always seem to have to tell people what they should do.

4) I am a serious and sober-minded person.

5) I am independent and self-sufficient in most things.

6) I am more of a thinker than an emotional person.

7) I am resourceful and practical.

8) I am the head of my household.

9) I am unsentimental at work.

10) I am very competitive.

11) I choose the clothes for my girlfriend - I know best what makes her look good.

12) I consider myself better than most other people that I meet.

13) I do not wear clothes that are too trendy or young for my age.

14) I enjoy giving other people the benefit of my knowledge and expertise.

15) I enjoy learning new things.

16) I get impatient with other people - they are so stupid sometimes.

17) I hate rules and regulations.

18) I have a passion for life and living.

19) I love games - sport, T.V. games, computer games and so on.

20) I love going out with my mates to the pub or club.

21) I often fool around - I have been told off about it.

22) I sometimes go into moods and sulks.

23) I take the leadership role when in a group of people.

24) I tell other people what to do because they can't sort it out themselves.

25) I think things through logically rather than allow my emotions to rule my head.

26) I use 'pet' names for my girlfriend - like 'baby' and so on.

27) I want the approval of my girlfriend.

28) Sometimes I feel helpless, needy and vulnerable.

29) The three best things in life are girls, football and parties.

30) Girls are best staying at home, cooking, dressmaking and looking after the house.

A quiz about how you see your female partner

1) I never seem able to please my girlfriend.

2) My girlfriend acts like a little princess - even like a spoiled brat.

3) My girlfriend always wants to organize me and find me jobs to do.

4) My girlfriend buys and wears new, fashionable clothes a lot.

5) My girlfriend does not want to take on responsibilities.

6) My girlfriend dresses quite plainly but smartly, reflecting her age.

7) My girlfriend enjoys being the center of attention a lot.

8) My girlfriend gives out insults and acidic comments.

9) My girlfriend has a very common sense approach to life.

10) My girlfriend has a very conventional sense of humor.

11) My girlfriend interferes in what other people are doing.

12) My girlfriend is attentive and always shows interest if I want to talk seriously.

13) My girlfriend is dependable, punctual and reliable.

14) My girlfriend is emotional - crying, tantrums, anger and so on.

15) My girlfriend is like a matron - condescending and patronizing.

16) My girlfriend is not a very emotional person.

17) My girlfriend is not overly concerned with jewelry or fashion trends.

18) My girlfriend is often critical of me.

19) My girlfriend is the head of my household.

20) My girlfriend is very vibrant, willful and full of energy.

21) My girlfriend is well educated, even intellectual, in her approach to life.

22) My girlfriend likes art, music and other cultural activities.

23) My girlfriend loves animals, pets and ponies.

24) My girlfriend loves rings, necklaces, earrings and other jewelry.

25) My girlfriend makes up her own mind about things.

26) My girlfriend points her finger at me and tells me what to do quite often.

27) My girlfriend sometimes thinks of males as being noisy, dirty and smelly.

28) My girlfriend thinks of herself as being superior to others.

29) My girlfriend treats me like a child.

30) My girlfriend wants to let her hair down and go to parties and nightclubs.

Analyze your scores

Your scores show how you and your girlfriend relate to each other and they reflect three positions – three perspectives, attitudes or viewpoints - called Parent, Adult and Child. We will look at these in a moment but for now, group your scores together like this:

For the statements on how you see *yourself*, group your scores like this -

Question numbers -

3, 8, 11, 12, 14, 16, 23, 24, 26, 30 – Your total score for these questions shows how much you adopt a Parent position.

1, 2, 4, 5, 6, 7, 9, 13, 15, 25 - Your total score for these questions shows how much you adopt an Adult position.

10, 17, 18, 19, 20, 21, 22, 27, 28, 29. - Your total score for these questions shows how much you adopt a Child position.

Your total scores

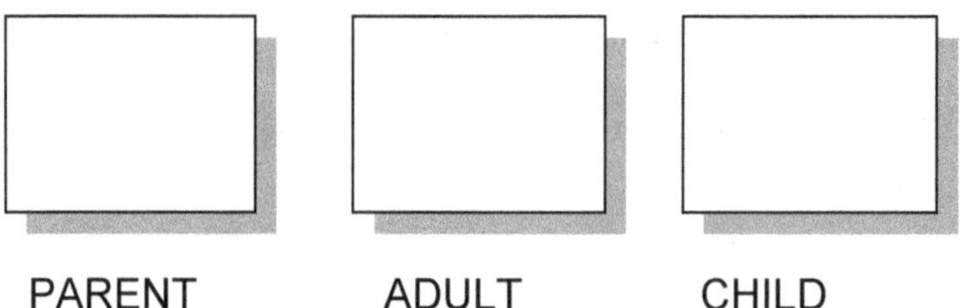

PARENT   ADULT   CHILD

Next look at the scores for how you rated the statements about how you see your GIRLFRIEND:

Question numbers -

1, 3, 8, 11, 15, 18, 19, 26, 28, 29 - Your total score for these questions shows how much you see your girlfriend being in her Parent position.

6, 9, 10, 12, 13, 16, 17, 21, 22, 25 - Your total score for these questions shows how much you see your girlfriend being in her Adult position.

2, 4, 5, 7, 14, 20, 23, 24, 27, 30. - Your total score for these questions shows how much you see your girlfriend being in her Child position.

Your total scores for your girlfriend

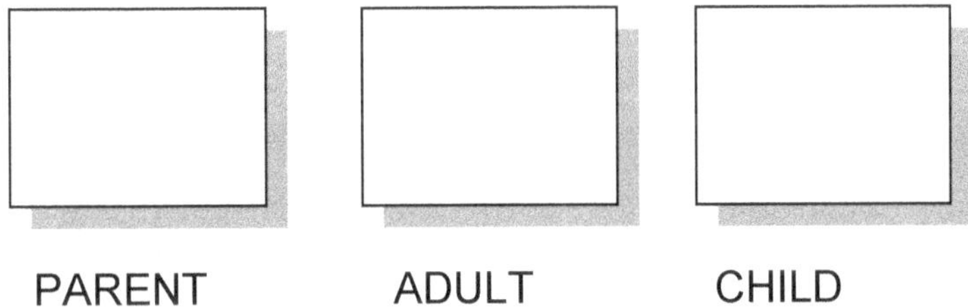

PARENT   ADULT   CHILD

Each of the Parent, Adult and Child scores in the two quizzes has a total limit of 50. You now have some idea of how these Parent, Adult and Child positions are distributed in terms of how you see yourself and how you see your girlfriend. Are they fairly equal, or does one of the positions score higher? Which is your strongest position? Which do you see as your girlfriend's strongest position?

First, time to relax! Take some time out before we move on to an explanation of what all this means.

2 MALES AMD FEMALES ARE DIFFERENT

You can't categorize differences between males and females using simple, clear-cut rules. Instead you have to talk about **tendencies**: *Most* females are not as strong as males, but *some* females succeed very well on the army front line, or as athletes – and *some* males make great fashion designers, dressmakers and wedding planners.

Some of the things we are going to look at won't apply to *your* girlfriend. That doesn't mean that what we say is false - it means your girlfriend does not follow this particular *trend*.

If it doesn't apply, ignore it

But it may well apply to your <u>next</u> girlfriend

1: We are physically different

Obvious huh? Males and females have biological and genetic differences. One obvious difference means that is important for you to be aware that some girlfriends can have a difficult time in the days leading up to their 'monthly period' or menstruation period – hence the term

'Pre-menstrual tension' or 'PMT'. Every twenty-eight days or so, for a few days, some girlfriends may become noticeably more irritable, tense, critical and sarcastic – even irrationally so, and they may be overly sensitive, irritable, prone to crying or easily be upset.

> **They can't help this any more than you can remove spots if you have measles**

It may well save some arguments if you become aware of these times so that you know when they are due to occur so you can be patient and understanding. Flag these times up in whatever you use for a personal diary or calendar.

2: A different balance of thoughts and feelings

Most girls function emotionally – based on how they feel right now. They may struggle to make detached, thoughtful, analytical evaluations of the world and relationships. Don't be critical - many males struggle to 'get in touch' with their feelings. This means that what *you* regard as important and what girlfriends regard as important are different - potentially causing problems in your relationships.

Males are concerned with Aggressiveness, Aloneness, Analysis, Building, Containment, Coolness, Courage, Encouragement, Explanation, Exploration, Faithfulness, Fatherhood, Final outcomes, Formality, Friendship, The Future, Goals, Guidance, Independence, Jobs to do, Knowledge, Leadership, Learning, Logic, Lustfulness, Schedules, Self-sufficiency, Separation, Sex, Stature, Study,

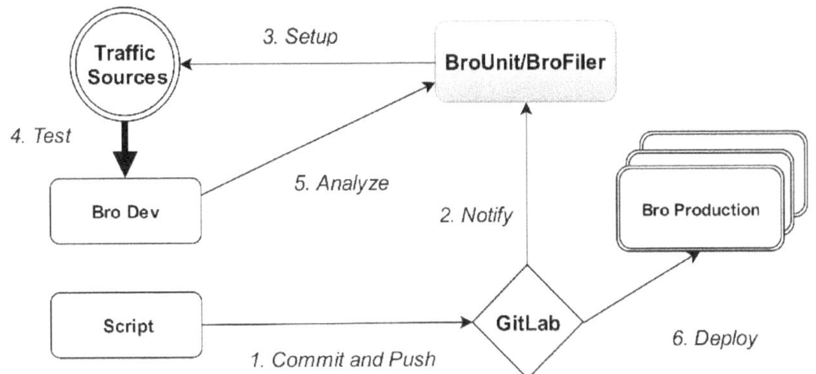

Targets, Teaching, Thinking, Time and Winning. Because they have a thoughtful approach to life, males produce theories, ideas and analysis of the world. They construct inner 'maps' to navigate the world based on concepts, ideas and categories.

By contrast, girls make sense of their world emotionally and are concerned with Belonging, Communion, Continuity, Cultivation, Emergence, Emotions, Feelings, Help, Inclusion, Inner Depths, Abandonment of thought, Motherhood, Natural cycles, Nearness, Nurturing, Passion, Peace, The Present Moment, Relationships, Seasons, Senses, Support, Tenderness, Union, Warmth and Working together.

Their emotions vary from moment to moment. What feels right today may not feel right tomorrow, so girls constantly seek to make sure that their 'felt sense' of the world  is correct. They seek to keep their sense of belonging and inclusion by sharing and confirming their 'felt sense' of the world with others, especially with females, because then they feel safe and secure. Girls make decisions and act in ways that make *emotional* sense to *them*, but these same decisions and behaviors can seem to be irrational, illogical or unreasonable to *males*.

3: Emotional intelligence

In explaining their behavior, girls use 'emotional intelligence'

'Us women are not always right but we are never wrong'

There is logic here captain, but not as we know it

'Emotional intelligence' is a *form* of thinking dominated by present moment emotions – leading to **'female logic'**. It is logical to the female because it is consistent with her feelings and emotions right now

Unfortunately for you, her feelings may well be hidden from sight for the most part, which means that you can't see the foundation of her 'logic'. This means that her decisions and conclusions seem illogical and contradictory to you.

'Emotional intelligence' is the BIG ONE

It's the one that males have most trouble with

Remember:

> Her decisions, opinions and behaviors – whether they seem logical or not to you - are *emotional* decisions, opinions and behaviors logically based on how she feels here and now

For example: *A female contestant in a quiz is asked: 'In what month is Armistice Day celebrated?' Typically, she thinks aloud – 'Hmmm. Armistice Day. That's something to do with flowers - Poppies I think. Oooo! I am not sure what month Armistice Day is in. I have three daughters and the youngest is named Poppy! She was born in February, so I think I will go with Armistice Day being in February.'*

You see – there *is* a form of logic – its just bollocks as far as males are concerned!

'Emotional intelligence' means that your girlfriend understands the world by using her **'felt sense'** –

> If she feels good about something then that something *is* good
>
> If she feels she dislikes something, then that something *is* bad

But -

Her 'felt sense' is not constant or consistent

Her 'understanding' of the world changes on the basis of how she feels at any given moment. If she feels threatened by a teenage boy who is walking down the street on his own, then he **is** a 'threatening' man or a 'bad' man.

During puberty, emotional turbulence will fill her brain – the world will feel like a very unpredictable place because her unpredictable emotions change from moment to moment.

Any attempts by you to use logic or provide analysis will sooner or later fall on deaf ears

Female: 'I can't take it in anymore, there's no room in my brain'

Male: 'That's because it's the size of a walnut and full of shit'

4: A different relationship to time - multi-tasking

Males are focused on the future. Look at supermarket shelf stackers. They have a certain number of product lines to stack on the shelves by a certain time. A male will focus on the 

future and ignore any distractions that may prevent him from reaching his target on time.

By contrast, girls focus on the present moment. Their attention is far broader than yours. Females see the gap on the shelf related to the products they are packing, but they also see a trolley full of different products next to this gap, ready to be stacked on other shelves. They merchandise the trolley stock, since this is ready now and right next to them at this moment, even though many of these products are *already* on the shelf and the product that they were packing still has an empty gap. Whilst merchandising these trolley products, they chat to customers nearby and at the same time they are aware that a fellow worker seems to be standing nearby doing nothing.

Females call this their ability to **multi-task** – a 'superior' ability to do more than one thing at a time – a 'skill' that they believe males have no ability in whatsoever.

'Can't you do two things at once? I thought you were more talented than that! What went wrong?'

So-called 'multi-tasking' is a myth invented and promoted by females who have little or no ability to focus on one task at a time, or to strategically plan for the future.

Your girlfriend may indeed be more aware than you are of what is happening just off to the side somewhere in the here and now –

But she works slower and makes more mistakes

These are 'multi-task failures'

Males look to the future and have laser - focused awareness

Females focus on the present-moment and have a wider scope of awareness

You will experience this in shopping trips. She will be present-moment centered and lots of items will catch her eye right now. You will be focused on the item you came into the shop for – that's the purpose of coming to the shop. She will sense your irritability and impatience - just over to her side - and complain that you are putting her on some sort of timetable or deadline. You just want to buy what you came into the shop for. If this gets bad enough you will both end up walking out of the shop in bad moods and without a purchase.

5: Different approaches to problem solving

Faced with problems, you want to find solutions. If your mate tells you he is not getting on with his boss, you will seek practical solutions. When your girlfriend says *she* is having problems with *her* boss, you will look for ways to solve her problem.

This is not what she wants

She wants someone to 'come alongside', listen to her and repeat to her what she is saying about how terrible she **feels** about her boss.

6: Different approaches to 'togetherness' – She needs to 'belong' and you want independence

Being included a group, especially a group of females, gives her reassurance and a feeling of safety. If your girlfriend feels *excluded* from a group she will feel uncomfortable, unsettled and vulnerable.

Her need to belong and be included is revealed when she makes statements that demand your agreement:

'The world is a terrible place, **yea**?'

'Those people across the road are nosey - **don't you think**?'

'There are too many immigrants in this country – **that's right isn't it**?'

These questions seem logical but in fact she is **expressing how she feels right now.** She makes sense of the world and relationships based on her 'feelings' or 'felt sense'.

'Belonging' to a group and 'sharing' helps her to confirm that her feelings are right or accurate. So girls huddle together, and often follow each other, or the 'mother hen', or just like little chicks.

If three girls go out together, none of them will want to leave to go home first because they know that the other two will then talk about her after she has gone. In the same way, when girls meet up for a meal, when they order the food, the following exchange is typical:

'What are **we** eating today?'

Or

1st F: 'What are you going to have?'

2nd F: 'I'll have what you are having.'

Your girlfriend will not want to exclude herself from such a female group by being seen to be different, independent or individual. She will sacrifice these qualities to keep her 'felt sense' of belonging. Some girls take this to an extreme and act like Lemmings. (Lemmings are small mammals that mindlessly follow other Lemmings such that the whole group jumps over the cliff to their deaths). These girls will 'cluck together like chicks' and may even dress the same as they all agree with and confirm one another's viewpoint. The 'Mother Hen' or Queen Bee may offer a new point of view and then they will all follow suit, because to be different is to commit an unforgivable sin and to encourage gossip.

If your girlfriend really is different, she is isolated from her own generation, her parent's generation and her children's generation – none of them will ever understand and she will always shock them. But some girls celebrate the fact that they are different, and their grandparents will be proud, and see their grandchild as a 'chip off the old block'. Her grandchildren will say, 'What a life she must have had!' and they will try and copy it.

Despite appearances, girls are not loyal to each other

If your relationship with your girlfriend begins to break up, and you are seen to be attractive by the other girls in her group, it may well be your soon-to-be-ex-girlfriend's 'best female friend' who will be the first to offer you 'comfort' behind her back - even before the relationship has finished.

…as though the boyfriend had no choice of his own.

A female's boyfriends are **trophies** that reflect her status in her group – ugly boyfriend = low status.

When her boyfriend is 'stolen' it lowers her status in the group

As your girlfriend encounters various 'crises' like this, you may come across **'all or nothing thinking'** or even fall into it yourself. With 'all or nothing thinking' there is no middle ground – no gray, only black or white – one extreme or another. It is classed as a dysfunctional thinking strategy.

F: 'I hate Gina – she changes people' [Felt sense]

As though people have no will of their own.

F: 'She changes *everyone*' [All or nothing thinking]

'All or nothing thinking' can sometimes be expressed as '*double* all or nothing thinking':

F: '*No one* knew *anything*'

Gina undermines your girlfriend's status level in her group and uses her fear of being excluded against her. Then Gina persuades another group member, Sophie, to take her side in a dispute. The female process of reasoning may look like this:

It can't possibly be my fault [All or nothing]

It can't be Sophie's fault because I *like* Sophie [Felt sense / Emotional intelligence]

Because I like Sophie she must also like me [Emotional intelligence]

It must be Gina's fault because she is the nearest available person that I do not feel that I like [Felt sense/Present moment awareness/Emotional intelligence]

You could logically analyze and challenge these statements with your girlfriend, and she may actually agree that:

She uses the same tactics that Gina uses

Other people do indeed have a mind of their own

It isn't 'everyone' that has changed, only Sophie

Despite her agreement, a few days later you may well have this conversation:

M: 'How are you getting on with Sophie?'

F: 'We never fell out!'

M: 'I thought you had.'

F: 'That was Gina'

Logical explanations are abandoned as your girlfriend habitually returns to 'feeling talk' – demonstrating a combination of:

Her need to belong

Present moment thinking

'Emotional intelligence'

All or nothing thinking

Girly groups

Girly group leaders - (Mother Hens and Queen Bees) - dominate by using their tone of voice or by being louder than others. In this way they control when others can speak, what the subject is and what the opinion of the group should be. Needing to belong and remain included, the other girls tend to follow her to avoid being isolated. (Queen Bees reflect a more 'superior', opinionated Critical Parent, rather than Bossy Child).

'Girly groups' members seek both attention and status within the group. If a girl member successfully obtains a new boyfriend she will show him off to the other 'chicks' so that she can say, 'Look what I caught!'. Members of 'girly groups' are overly concerned with what other people are doing both in and out of the group, and they don't want to appear to be too different from other group members and run the risk of being pulled apart by them and being isolated.

You have no status with or loyalty from these girls. They are likely to kick you when you are down. When you are suffering with a cold, these girls will dismiss any *male* suffering, and imply that all

males fake their condition and that they are wimps.

You can deal with criticism by '**fogging**'

'Fogging' means that you agree with *anything* that is possibly, relatively or probably true. If you throw a ball into the fog it disappears – it is not thrown back. That is how you act when 'fogging'. For example:

> F: 'Oooohhh! He's suffering from 'man-'flu!''

> (In dismissive, put-down tones)

> M: *'That's right.* 'Man-'flu' is the worst kind

> - You girls wouldn't know anything about it.'

In response to the statement:

> 'You are an idiot'

You can reply

> 'That's true, I am an idiot.'

…because when compared to Einstein, most of us are idiots. So when an insult or criticism is thrown at you, instead of catching it and throwing it back - or making the situation worse by finding a bigger insult or criticism to throw back - you absorb the insult / criticism and by doing so show that such things don't bother you at all. All that you do is merely 'mirror' or reflect back what the person has said and put 'That's true' or 'You're right' in front of it:

> F: 'You're clumsy'

M: 'That's true, I am clumsy.'

This approach also works with praise:

F: 'You are very clever!'

M: 'You are right! I am clever!' (Good girl for noticing)

Males are excluded from 'girly groups'

Unless they are:

Really desirable, or

Clearly gay or effeminate

Girly-group members make statements like: 'He's a man! What would he know?' They exclude males so that they can talk about female concerns. If you are within listening distance, the girly group will break up and move away - this is girl-talk. **FACT**: you don't want to be involved in 'girly groups'. They talk about obstetrics, gynecology, scandals, fashions, what people are doing, wearing, eating and thinking, where they are living, domestic arrangements, menopause, health, hospital operations, children, washing powder, meal deals, how many clothes the children wear each day, the latest romantic fiction and so on.

You don't want to have to listen to this crap. You want to get away to your car, football, games console, local bar, flying your drone or whatever. Since these girls don't want male company either, this arrangement suits both parties.

'Girly groups' are sustained by Diet clubs, Aerobic classes,

Line dancing, Sequence dancing, Gym fitness classes, Mother's meetings, Ladies church fellowship meetings, the Women's Institute, Young mum's coffee mornings, Young wives weekly or monthly trips to restaurants, Synchronized swimming, Cheerleader groups, Dancing troops and so on.

These activities often involve **going through a set of actions all together at the same time.** This gives a feeling of togetherness, connection and belonging – so they are activities that meet the emotional needs of many girls.

7: Different parenting skills: Motherhood

'My boyfriend is house trained'

Motherhood is a primary female role concerned with bringing forth, sustaining and developing life. Females who reach adolescence and beyond may become 'brooding' -they have a longing to be fulfilled mothers.

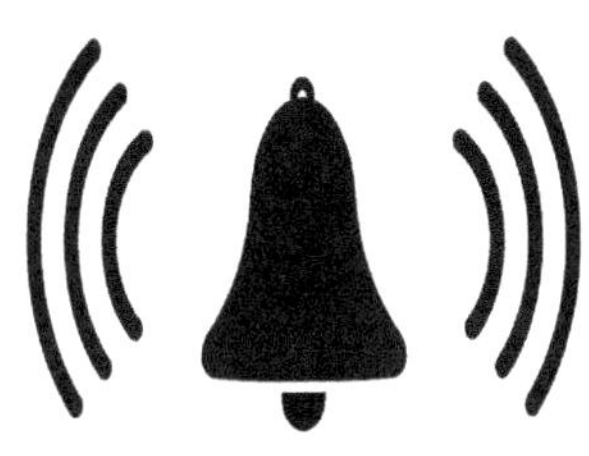

WARNING!!! Your girlfriend may give you a lot of attention so she can reach her ultimate emotional satisfaction of becoming pregnant. When the baby is born, all her attention will be on her baby, to your exclusion.

The 'Empty nest' syndrome

A Mother knows that one day her children will 'fly the nest'. This can lead to 'empty nest syndrome' - her deep sense of loss regarding her purpose, meaning and identity coupled with a feeling of emptiness and aloneness.

If you have a relationship with a mature female, she may try to extend her 'mother' role by treating you like a child in need of mothering.

Home is the 'nest' that she seeks to build. She will spend a great deal of time attending to this 'nest' - cleaning it, maintaining it and making sure that it is presented in a 'correct' and acceptable way. Her concerns center on the home much more than yours.

8: A different reward system

Be very clear about the female reward system. Males allocate a **range** of 'reward points' based on the difficulty of the task and/or the length of time that the task takes to be done. Remembering to pick up lottery tickets might earn one or two points, but cutting the lawn might earn five points because it is a bigger task. Decorating a room might get ten to twenty points and so on.

This is NOT how females work

> Females give EVERYTHING ONE point!

Wash the dishes - 1 point

Decorate a room - 1 point

Get her car serviced - 1 point

Risk life to adjust the T.V. Antenna - 1 point

Doing her an unasked for favor - 

WARNING!
Females keep score

Not only does she note and score every favorable task that you do, (with 1 point) – **but she notes every mistake and failure of yours too.**

When girlfriends misbehave, males just tend to 'let it go' – and her mistakes get forgotten.

But there is a double whammy

Females not only *remember* every one of <u>your</u> misbehaviors, shortcomings and mistakes -

> *Females conveniently <u>forget</u> their own misbehavior, shortcomings and mistakes*

These are some of the differences between males and females that are the root causes of problems in your relationship with your girlfriend. How can you deal with these problems in practical ways? First you need a theoretical approach to guide your behaviour and attitude. This is the theme of the next chapter.

But first, take a break

Hopefully, you have answered all the questions in the quiz and scored your answers

IF NOT, DO IT NOW!

Each of your answers was placed into one of three positions -

Parent, Adult or Child

These are the ideas that we will use in understanding your relationship with your girlfriend. I will write these categories like this: 'Parent', 'Adult' and 'Child' - using capital letters. 'Parent', 'Adult' and 'Child' refer to positions that people take in their relationships – they are three viewpoints that people adopt when they relate to others – and that you can adopt when you relate to your girlfriend.

Let's look at each one in more detail. As we do, keep in mind how much you and your girlfriend fit into these three categories based on your quiz scores.

Parent

People in Parent position act like Parents. (Surprise!!). If a person you are relating to is in their Parent position, they act as if you are like a child and they are your 'superior' supervisor. We all adopt a Parent position at times. We draw out this position from our childhood views of our own parents and caregivers. We may have one Parental viewpoint drawn from our mother, another from our father and others drawn from teachers and so on.

Adult

A person in Adult position acts like a mature adult and applies common sense problem-solving strategies, reasons things through logically and is able ask for help from others. Such a person is centered in the present and has feelings in response to what's happening here and now. Their behavior is consistent with how they think and feel.

Child

A person in Child position acts like a 'big kid' one way or another. This 'Inner Child' is drawn from the person's own childhood memories that have been stored *at the processing and functioning level of a child.* The Child position is connected to fun, pleasure, adventure, rebellion, naughtiness and rule breaking. So people tend to have an obedient Child, naughty Child, rebellious Child and so on.

People constantly change their position

When a person is seeing the world and operating from one of these viewpoints, we say that they are 'in Parent', or 'in Adult' or 'in Child' – for shorthand. People are not purely Adult, Parent or Child all the time, but have a constantly changing mixture. We are PAC man (and woman). There is

no particular position that you should try to be in all the time. We move quickly from one position to another – from Parent to Child and back again in the time it takes to speak three sentences. But we do tend to naturally settle in or prefer one position or another. Even so, our position changes depending on

The position of the person we are relating to and

The situation we are in.

Some people bring out the Child in us, others bring out the Adult and yet others the Parent, and situations also affect our position. For example when someone is physically hurt when we are fooling around, we quickly come out of Child into Adult or Parent.

Inner conflict

Our Parent, Adult and Child positions have contradictions and inconsistencies between themselves and these can cause conflicts within us. For example, I decide to start a diet because it's healthy and good for me [Adult] but next day I am tempted to have my favorite take-away [Child], putting me in conflict with my earlier [Adult] decision to start a diet.

People in relationship

When people relate to each other, each of them are in Parent, Adult or Child. For example, one person may be critical and use an authoritative tone of voice - Critical Parent. We may react to them by becoming very angry at being spoken to like a child, and we may stamp our feet and have a tantrum – we respond in our Angry Child.

> *Any combination of positions*
>
> *may occur in a relationship*

For example, instead of angry Child, we could respond as Critical Parent and start to tell *them* what *they* 'should', 'ought' and 'must' do and say. This turns the relationship into a Critical Parent/Critical Parent interaction, rather than Critical Parent/Angry Child interaction.

Crossed relationships

You may want to be spoken to like an Adult but the person you are talking to insists on being Parental, relating to you as if you are an immature Child – and you feel belittled. This becomes a 'crossed interaction' or 'crossed relationship'.

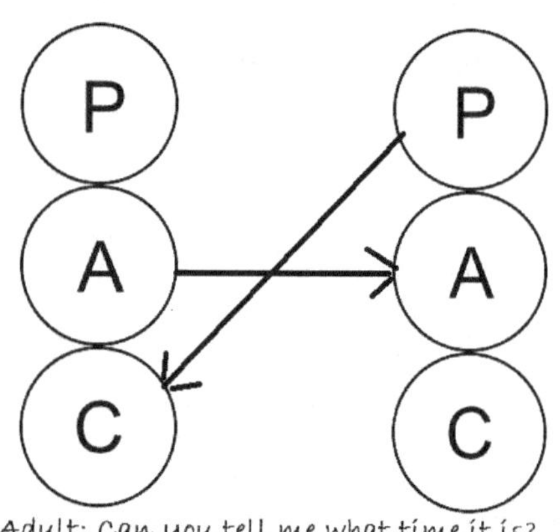

Adult: Can you tell me what time it is?
Critical Parent: You are always late.

Your options: Do as you are told [Obedient Child]; Refuse to do what they say, stamping your feet [Rebellious Child]; Talk to them in a mature, reasoned way [Adult]; or say 'Who do you think you are' telling *them* what *they* 'ought' to do [Parent].

If you move to Adult position and try to suggest good reasons for your behavior as a defense against their criticism, the person may carry on in Parent position and cut across your logic using 'superior', louder tones of voice because they 'know better'. You will be one down. If you allow them to place you in Child position you will be led by your feelings rather than your logic, and you will react emotionally and childishly – and they will keep their 'superiority', control and 'authority'. You will be two down.

Let's look at these three positions more closely.

Adult

Males *and* females in Adult position act their age and have a responsible, common sense approach, using logic and analysis to help their decision-making, target setting and problem solving in an appropriate way. They get information, learn and then share their knowledge and experience to find practical solutions. They take responsibility for what they do or do not do as they choose their own actions. They are not particularly emotional – they are serious, practical and responsible, and what humor there is will be very conventional. But they don't keep telling other people what to do unless they are in an official role of supervisor or boss.

A person in Adult position is revealed by their attentiveness and interest. They are non-threatening and non-threatened and use words like - 'why', 'what', 'how', 'who', 'where' and 'when'; 'how much', 'in what way', 'true', 'false', 'probably', 'possibly', 'I think', 'I realize', 'I see', 'I believe' or 'in my opinion', all of these being coupled with reasoned, logical statements.

But, since males and females are different there are gender differences in the Adult position

The male Adult

As you mature into your late teens and early twenties, in your Adult position you will be masculine, independent, self-sufficient and stand alone from others. It will not matter to you what others think of you or your opinions. You will take responsibility for your own decisions, and not be ashamed of what you do. Polite and well mannered, especially with ladies, you will be a thinker and planner, good with your hands, and look down on those who give in to social trends and rules. Speaking the truth, you may sometimes be callous and unpredictable, but you will see both sides of a situation whilst having a definite opinion of your own. Humor will not be your strong point - you may be quite serious. You will not be sly or underhanded at work but straightforward, honest, resourceful, practical and unsentimental. You will dress sensibly in clothes that reflect your age and the task at hand.

You will not be underhanded with girlfriends either, but be very straightforward with them and protective of her well-being. You will not want limit her freedom - rather, you will want her to reach her full potential. You may buy her gifts and clothes but be more likely to give your responsible [Adult] girlfriend your credit card suggesting that she treat herself to something she feels comfortable in.

If you scored highest in the Adult category in the quiz, then this description will tend to fit your approach to life and to females.

The Female Adult

Adult is the least emotional of the three positions and has an emphasis on thought, responsibility and common sense. Females in Adult can appear boring to you, as well as to other females and even herself. But it is a huge mistake to think that she is not intelligent. She is quite capable of running a business - probably better than most males. Straightforward, honest - even ruthless - in making business deals, if you find this out in the real world, you may become disillusioned. If she is more

assertive than you and done better than you, your instinct may be to want to unfairly 'punch below the belt' by accusing her of suffering from pre-menstrual tension. This is because you feel her deflating your male pride very strongly.

A female in Adult is self-reliant, not turning to her parents or to substitute parents - she behaves in a mature, dignified, responsible but feminine way and is considered to be a real 'Lady', earning and gaining the respect of both males and females.

Although looking rather plain, she is still feminine even though she may not be interested in jewelry or the latest fashions, and is likely to dress in sensible but smart feminine clothes. She is not overly interested in the latest hair fashions either, though her hairstyle looks smart and feminine. She does not need to attract attention to herself by being loud either in the way she speaks or dresses, or by throwing tantrums. She has an air of quietness about her, being modest in public, timid when it comes to raising her voice and she may sometimes blush.

Reliable and punctual, she will be a valued employee - perhaps a personal secretary to a boss. She may see the best in others and be kind, sincere, trusting, optimistic, gentle, tenderhearted, unselfish and loyal - but she *does* live in the real world and she is well able to make sharp evaluations of what other people are like.

She makes up her own mind rather than following rumors or gossip and tends not to be a gossip herself, nor a 'girly-girl' within a female group. She is self-possessed, in control of herself and does not engage in silly 'giggling', is not afraid of the dark and does not descend into helpless panic if she is lost in dense fog. She celebrates life from an informed point of view and in a crisis she is strong – tireless in soothing the sadness of others.

At parties she may seem like a wallflower, but is busy making sure that all the practical details are being attended to and everything is running smoothly. She may dance, but only after the party has been a success, and most likely dances with her boyfriend in a dignified way - she is unlikely to show displays of passion or emotion in public. She is the supporting strength of her male partner and always tends to be at his side as a sword, shield, comfort and strength to her male partner and her close family.

She does not criticize or exclude males; regard them as 'dirty, smelly boys'; or treat them in a condescending way. She meets males as equals - unless they make the mistake of being immature or 'superior' to her.

Do you see your girlfriend as scoring high in the Adult category in the quiz?

Parent

Both males and females in Parent assume an unasked for 'supervisory' role over other people, wanting to change how other people speak and act. They use 'parental' words, coupled with the tone, pitch and loudness of their voice and 'supervisory', 'superior' body language, to display their sense of their own 'superiority' and 'higher wisdom'. They expect respect and obedience, and by their manner they suggest that other people are 'inferior', irresponsible, 'inadequate' or just plain stupid. So they give orders ('Stop giggling!'), and presume an authority role: ('I hope you behaved!'). Other people see them as interfering busybodies, controlling, manipulative or arrogant. They can be very critical and sarcastic: ('What small part of your brain came to life just then?'). They often constantly point to the other person's failure: ('You did quite a good job. Pity you didn't finish it completely. But then you never do, do you?'). By treating other people like children they often bring out that person's Defiant, Naughty Child, or the Sneaky, Underhanded Child. They may also bring out the other person's Obedient Child – who always seeks to gain the approval of this 'Parental' person, though they will rarely, if ever, succeed.

The words: 'should', 'ought' or 'must' indicate that a person is in their Parent position. Other key words and phrases include: 'always', 'never', 'once and for all', judgmental words, expressions of disappointment or disapproval and moralizing. Physical clues include: impatient body language, finger-pointing and 'superior' gestures such as standing to their full height with their hands on their hips.

If you hear yourself saying things that your mother or father used to say to you when they were telling you off – especially if you are speaking to your girlfriend - you are in your Parent position.

If this was your largest score in the quiz, then you may find that you adopt your Parent position by default - as your *regular* and *habitual* position when you relate to other people, especially females.

Parental males *and* females can be pompous, affronted, disappointed, disapproving, loud and overbearing such that they shout others down and interrupt others when they are speaking. They seem confident, critical and superior.

The male Parent

Males in Parent are father-like, and take people 'under their wing' to protect, nurture and guide them. His home is his castle and he is of the view that his female partner should be guided by his 'superior' knowledge, accept his opinions in full, and have no opinions of her own. He tolerates what he sees as her foolish ideas but may criticize her as if she is a little girl for her stupidity and especially her arrogance if she oversteps the mark and tries to act like an independent Adult. He wants her to stay at home like females 'should'. She has to hand over any money she earns to him as the 'superior' manager of their finances. You may laugh, but this is by no means uncommon in certain religious circles for example, where males are regarded as the head of the household and females are meant to obey.

He will not change his behavior to suit others - especially his girlfriend. If he swears and smokes he will continue to do so at home. She will have to get used to his 'bad' habits as she calls them. This is the price she pays for the privilege of being with him. He may supervise her choice of clothes and throw away items of her clothing that he thinks are unsuitable, without asking her first. He orders their food in restaurants because he knows what to order, how it should be cooked and what wine goes with what food, much better than she does. He doesn't explain his actions to her at all. He uses parental language - 'My dear', 'sweetheart', 'honey', 'babe' and so on, placing her in Child position. In fact he may be particularly attracted to females in their Child position – especially obedient Child - because he can then adopt various father-like roles with her of Protector, Rescuer, Disciplinarian or Teacher.

But it would be a mistake for him to think that all females are 'silly little things'. When he *seriously* says something like 'Don't worry your pretty little head about.....', he reveals his own superficial understanding of females.

When a female in Adult is successful at work or business, it is a shock to his male pride and he finds her difficult to deal with. On the other hand, if she is unsuccessful in her business ventures, this allows him to be 'superior' and say - 'Poor, sweet, silly girls - they try very hard. They can think that they are helping - until a real man comes along to relieve them of their burdens and concerns'.

The female Parent

> *Women can't do it themselves, but they are always there*
>
> *to tell others that they are doing it incorrectly*

Many females – whatever their age – have strong 'motherly' instincts. Some find 'child substitutes' - a pet dog overly pampered, dressed up and spoken to like a baby, **OR** a male partner to be mothered and nurtured – fussed over one moment and despised the next for being so helplessly and hopelessly childish instead of being a man.

Some females are almost always Parental towards their boyfriends

Females in Parent – even young females - act like 'mother', even though the person that they 'mother' - AND IT COULD BE **YOU** - has not asked for such 'supervision'. They organize which adult is sitting where at the dinner table even though they have not been asked to do so. They are like 'matrons' taking charge and setting the agenda, often by subtle means or sometimes by not so subtle means. She will tidy up your apartment without being asked to do so, throw away items in your house because she thinks they are no longer of use or fashionable, disapprove of your lifestyle and start issuing orders as she assumes the role of being in charge because 'she knows best'.

Females in Parent are revealed by:

Pushing in or not giving way to others

Ridiculing the opinions of others

Being louder than others

Interrupting when others are speaking

Standing in a doorway causing an

obstruction

Taking up lots of room where she is

working causing an obstruction

Adopting an 'I am in charge' tone of

voice - as self-appointed leader

Setting the theme of conversations

Being quick to disapprove of any child-

like outbursts of behavior - especially

from males.

'I'll be round there to you men to smack some legs in a minute!'

The 'Foster Mother' Parent

There is a difference between nurturing a six-year-old son and a sixteen-year-old male. Mom can tell you what to eat when you are six, but not when you are twenty-six! You have boundaries and they change as you become mature. Females in Parent fail to recognise or respect these boundaries and cross your boundary lines!

Such a female will tell you what you 'should', 'ought' and 'must' do, expect you to show her respect, and do as you are told, not answering back. She takes away your ability to exercise self-control and independence as a mature adult – she will slowly but surely emasculate you. She *fosters* your dependent Childish position.

For example, you arrive at a self-service restaurant:

F: 'You sit there. I'll get your lunch' [Female Parent]

M: 'Don't put too many potatoes on, just a few carrots and a little gravy' [Male Obedient Child]

See? She puts you in a childish role, telling you where to sit and in effect to sit still and be quiet. She takes control of getting your food so you have to go into detail about what you do and do not want on your plate instead of acting in your Adult position and getting it for yourself.

Now you may be attracted by this behavior at first because you like being made a fuss of – (You are already in Child). You like being 'mothered' [by her Parent] a little bit. But if this carries on you may even end up asking her 'What shall I wear?' 'What do I want to eat?' or even 'What do *you* think *mother*?' - using 'mother' as your 'pet name' for her. And she will indeed tell you what to wear, what to eat, how much to eat, where to sit, what to say and when to say it. She will override your likes and dislikes – ('I know you did not want any carrots but I've put some on your plate anyway because they are good for you.'). She will give out orders to you as if she is speaking to a naughty child: ('Take your shoes off before coming in here!') or she will demand explanations: ('Where have you been 'til now?').

She may see this as caring, nurturing, helping, supporting and encouraging you because of her love for you. She may not understand what's happening when you express anger at being treated like a three year old all the time.

Your annoyance is the result of this 'crossed relationship' – where she insists on treating you like a Child and you want to be treated like an Adult.

There are at least two types of foster-mother girlfriend:

The '**Critical**' foster-mother girlfriend and

The '**Nurturing**' foster-mother girlfriend

A: 'Critical' Female Parent

The Critical Foster-Mother Parent is about empowerment and control - *her* empowerment and control over *you*. What you do will never be good enough or right. **You** will never be good enough. You will find yourself confused by her contradictory demands that are based on her present moment emotional needs that neither you nor anybody else can fathom out. She will insist on seeing you as Child, and your attempts at self-assertion or independence as defiant disobedience, leading to more authoritarian controlling behavior from her as she seeks to keep her control over you. She may even become slightly violent.

Violence and swearing are the last resorts of a desperate or defeated female

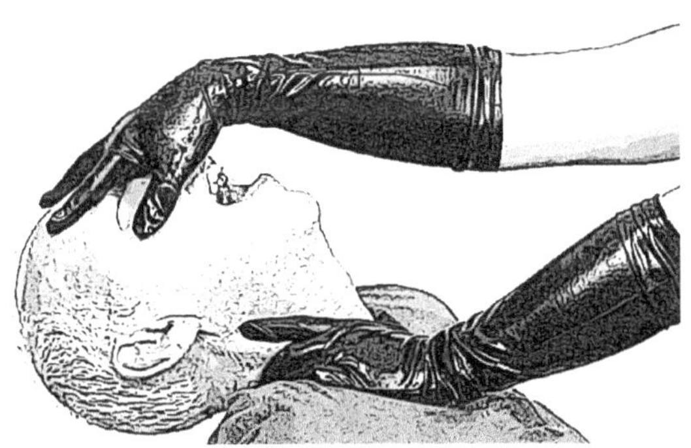

Her criticism will not be softened by warm laughter or generous smiles:

> M: 'If males are so attractive, why marry them?' [Male Adult]

> F: ' Because we feel sorry for them. In any case, I have a dog now - he does as he's told and is much more affectionate.' [Female Critical Parent]

B: 'Nurturing' Female Parent

The 'nurturing' female Parent sees herself as loving, supportive, helping and including. She will make you feel trapped and controlled. If you question or deny her, she will quickly move to **Critical** Parent – or move to Child and turn on her 'emotional tap'.

The smell of baking fills the house:

> M: 'Been baking?' [Male Adult]

> F: 'Yes, scones, but you can't have one. They're for your mum. [Female Parent nurturing your mom]

The male got out of this:

> M: 'Well I *am* having one.' [Flat contradiction, takes control back to himself - Male Parent] 'You're not giving my mum something that I've not tasted first!' [Humor softens his contradiction as he eats a scone]

But an opposite reaction may occur:

> M: 'Been baking?' [Male Adult]

> F: 'Yes, scones. I've made them all for you' [Female Parent. Unasked for nurturing]

Silence follows, as you make no attempt to eat a scone.

> F: 'Don't you want one? They're all for you' [Female Parent. Unasked for nurturing]

> M: 'No, not at the moment' [Male Adult]

> F: 'They're best when warm!' [Female Parent Persistent unasked for nurturing]. 'What's wrong with them?' [Edging to Critical Female Parent if said in an

'authoritarian' tone of voice, or Child if said in a 'hurt' voice]

Her unasked for nurturing puts you in a corner. Refuse it and you are asked to explain yourself [Female Parent] or made to feel guilty for upsetting her [Female Child]

> # Both 'Nurturing' *and* 'Critical' female
> # Parents rob you of your self-control

But at the end of the day, she wants a **man**, not a Child, even though she is turning you into a 'little boy' and will soon complain about your lack of manhood and despise you as a result. She will increasingly treat you with sarcastic contempt using phrases like:

'Him? He doesn't know his ass from his face!' [Critical Parent]

By robbing you of your self-control, females in Parent position cross your personal boundaries. There is an unasked for invasion of your privacy, authority and personal space as they step in where they are better holding back, and speak, giving opinionated advice when they are better remaining silent. Females in Parent seek to take charge of you and supervise you either in a 'superior' way or in a claustrophobic 'caring' way.

Female Parent and your vanity

If you boast about your sexual skills – (a male Child activity best avoided), females in Parent will respond to take you down a peg or two:

> F: 'If he spends a night with me he'll be in hospital for a month' [Female Parent]

Or a female friend in Parent may boast on her behalf:

> F: 'If Anne gets hold of you it'll take you a week to recover. She'll sort you out' [Female Parent]

If you boast about your sexual activity, sexual conquests, the size of your cock and so on then be prepared to have your bluff called. The rule is –

> NEVER MAKE ANY STATEMENTS ABOUT YOUR SEXUAL LIFE THAT YOU ARE NOT PREPARED TO BACK UP

So you call her bluff in return -

> M: 'When do you fancy trying to sort me out then? I fancy a stay in hospital' [Male Parent]

How far you are prepared to go in these kinds of challenges is up to you, but know your limits beforehand and be prepared to continue up to your limit until she backs down. Be prepared to do what you say and call her bluff in front of others who can see her back down. Then you will be one up, and can point out that she is 'all talk'.

Child

Both males and females in Child position want to let go of the limits and restrictions of their Parental and Adult positions. They want to play for a while, or to rebel and to do this they go into Child, the most emotional of the three positions.

Clues that reveal that a person is in Child position include - sad expressions, despair, temper tantrums, stamping of feet, whining voices, rolling eyes, shrugging of shoulders, teasing, delight, laughter, speaking behind their hand, raising their hand to speak or giggling. Phrases include 'I wish', 'I dunno', 'I want', 'I'm gonna', 'oh no', 'not again', 'things never go right for me', 'worst day of my life', 'bigger', 'biggest', 'best' and other superlatives used to impress. Their tone of voice is child-like.

The male Child

If a mature male wants to relax and have fun, he tends to adopt his Child position. In Child position males go into the emotional realm. Society encourages older males to control, hide or even suppress public displays of their emotions, especially their vulnerable emotions. If you cry or show fear you will be thought of as a wimp, weak or a 'big kid'. People in Parent may tell you to 'Grow up' or 'Be a man' and some females in Parent will despise your emotional displays and despise **you**, because you are not acting like a man, but like a Child.

Commonly seen male Child positions include the obedient, rule-following, good little boy, who needs and constantly seeks approval from significant others who are in Parent and Adult positions; the adventurous, risk-taking fun loving boy, the playful boy who wants to play games - electronic or otherwise; the mischievous, silly joker; the still immature but bossy group leader; the defiant, willful, obstinate boy; the highly competitive, must-win-at-any-cost boy; the moody, sulking boy; the angry, aggressive, bullying, violent boy; the naughty, misbehaving rebel; the passionate, energetic, vibrant boy; the remorseful, apologetic, confessing boy and the sneaky, underhanded, secretive tell-tale little boy. All of these can be seen at different times and situations in fully-grown males.

Females don't usually find the male Child position to be attractive in the main, feeling that such behavior shows off male immaturity – though such a male may make them laugh and have fun for a while.

Males in Child wear football t-shirts – with bulging beer-belly underneath, dress like teenagers and wear t-shirts with slogans like - 'This is what perfection looks like', or 'The best three things in life are girls, football and parties'. They joke and fool around in mock fights, coupled with shouting, chanting and loud laughter with their mates. The 'boys gang' is now lifted up to a football team Supporters Club or something similar. They want to go out clubbing, to football matches, to the local bar to get drunk or play electronic games. When males in Child play with techno gadgets such as Play Station, females call such devices 'Little boys toys'. The 'boys gang' goes out to nightclubs, strip joints, sporting events and bars for drinking sessions.

But if a man's strength and masterful qualities desert him, or if he is overwhelmed by tragic life events, he may collapse into his Child and suddenly be put in touch with his own fallibility, helplessness, need, failure and vulnerability – (all childhood emotions). He will become a man in need of his mother - or substitute mother - to whom he can confess. He may become tearful, sobbing, and feel sorry for himself, full of self-reproach - broken and helpless, eaten up by feelings of guilt or failure.

The female Child

Females hate being treated like children, especially by males, so they try to establish their own control,

independence, 'superiority' and authority over guys. But when it comes to romance, they want to be fussed over like a fairy princess. A female in Child is full of vanity and wants to feel that she is the top girl, the most attractive girl in the group – in town, in the world, wanting all the attention for herself. She functions emotionally – and this is a double whammy for you because even though her Adult and Parent positions are grounded in the emotional realm, her Child is the position where she is most in touch with and dominated by her feelings.

Common female Child behaviors include: the obedient, good little girl; giggling 'girly-girls' who exclude 'dirty, smelly boys'; girly-group group leaders who, though immature, act like a classroom monitor, bossy leader, rule enforcer and tell-tale to teacher. [In these cases the 'teacher' will be a nearby Parent figure]. The defiant, willful, obstinate little madam – (never argue with a female in her willful Child position), the moody, sulking, pouting spoiled brat; the foot stamping little princess given to tantrums, pinching people's skin, throwing things and crying; the naughty, misbehaving rebel; the passionate, energetic, vibrant girl; the vulnerable, crying, tearful-but-manipulative little girl; and the sneaky, underhanded, secretive, lying little girl.

Females in Child still need their parents or Parental substitutes – a Parental mother for emotional security and a Parental father for protection and rescuer when she ends up out of her depth or lost.

She passionately desires things and/or people but when she gets them, they lose their value so she then passionately desires something or someone else. She is headstrong, vain and insensitive and will use your love for her against you, seeing your love as weakness. Never let a female to tends to be in Child know that you love her or else she will despise and use you for her own purposes.

If she simply expresses her passionate desire she may feel that she has gained her desired object. She may believe her fantasy and then project it onto the person she craves:

> F: 'I love him therefore he must love me!' [Female Child. Emotional Intelligence].

She fantasizes that he loves her - therefore he must love her in reality. A female functioning from her Child position will provide you with the strongest demonstration of 'Emotional Intelligence' - all of her 'logic' follows on from her emotions. She has schoolgirl-like crushes, fantasies about male 'hunks', worships celebrities and has fantasies about real but unattainable male friends.

She loves parties, dancing, dressing up, new clothes, being treated like a Princess, having lots of baubles, bangles and beads, wearing makeup and having her hair fashionably cut. She loves dolls, babies, pets, ponies and presents. She will use whatever tactic works to get her own way and will lie, cry, be manipulative, playful, happy, sweet, thoughtful, angry, critical or attentive. She may be sneaky and go behind your back, scheming and planning and so be insincere, hypocritical and two-faced. She can be very spiteful and have a malicious, small-minded desire to harm or humiliate:

> F: 'Did you hear about the wedding? The groom's brother died that very afternoon. That will stop them from having a good time!' [Spiteful Child]

Very often she will state what is *really* on her mind or ask what she *really* wants in her **third** question in a verbal exchange:

> Statement 1) 'Is there much work to do today?'

> Statement 2) 'I think that this place needs tidying up.'

> **Statement 3) 'Who is in charge today?' (She wants to know so that she can do a lot of talking if the manager [Substitute Parent] is away).**

To try and get what she wants she may put on a helpless, dependent, pleading child-like victim attitude and voice:

> F: 'Miiiike...I don't know what to do!' [Helpless Child pleading voice]

Or, in a simpering, whimpering voice -

> F: 'Can we (I) have some more......[wine, gold rings, a new car]? [Child]

Or, in the same voice:

> F: 'What are you going to buy me?' [Child]

Or even:

F: 'What am I worth? [Child]

While she speaks like this she may stroke your arm and pout her lips so that you will be her rescuer, protector and provider.

Young boys want to play soldiers, be astronauts, climb trees, explore railway tunnels, and rebel against their parent's instructions. They don't want girls around because girls hold them back, criticize them and remind them of their parent's restrictive rules and go back home telling tales.

Little girls are thought of as 'sugar and spice and all things nice' as they play 'house' with soft toys and dolls and dismiss boys as too rough, dirty, sweaty, smelly and noisy. In a similar way, females in Child may still dismiss boys as too rough, dirty, sweaty, smelly and noisy, and they are much happier playing 'house'. As grown ups they are interested in flowers, décor, soft furnishings and other aspects of the home and criticize males as 'Boys playing with boy's toys' but the girly-girl [Child] equivalent of 'boys with boy's toys' is her home that has become her new 'doll's house'.

Girly-girl groups are made up of females in Child position with their voices raised in pitch to little-girl tones and lots of giggling and despising of males. There are lots of outraged 'Oooohhh's' and 'Aaaahhh's', nudging of elbows and whispering in huddles with hands covering mouths coupled with side-glances.

The whole group, including leader, is in Child position

The 'girly-girl' leader may say to the others:

> 'What's he doing now?'

Or

> 'Who does he think he is?'

Or

> 'He never answers the phone! I'll get it moved and put right by him so he *has* to answer it' [Bossy Child]

The others cluck in approval. Although their leader acts like a Parent – at the top of the pecking order, issuing commands to the others like a Parent - she is really the female Bossy Child playing Parent - a Child in charge of Children.

Female Bossy Child and Female Parent

Female Parent and Bossy Child are closely related

As the boyfriend of a female in either Parent or 'Bossy' Child, both you and your hobbies and interests will be dismissed. If you create something masculine – such as a working model steam engine – such females will damn it with faint praise -

F: 'Very good. Now clean yourself up and come in for tea!' [Nurturing Parent]

Or you yourself will be totally dismissed:

F: 'What do you think you are doing in here hour after hour playing with toy trains?' [Critical Parent]

Female Bossy Child and female Parent are difficult to tell apart - they are both 'bossy'. But bossy Child reveals herself in her emotive 'Little Princess', 'Little Madam', 'Spoiled Brat', and falsely parental 'Classroom Monitor' and 'Tell-tale to teacher'. A female in Child tries to use false authority to get her own way and be the center of attention, whereas female Parent is revealed when she assumes to take charge of both males *and* females as an over-nurturing, over-critical and sarcastic 'Supervisor', treating males *and* females with disdain and dismissal. As Parent and bossy Child, she over extends her importance and 'superiority'. If she is faced with rational, logical reasons that are different from her own opinions she believes that her years of experience mean that she knows better.

Fortunately you don't have to worry about trying to tell these two positions apart - your response to both of them will be the same

Learning to know yourself and others

You can now learn to be aware of people's positions. Begin to watch and listen to people relating to one another and try picking out whether they are in their Parent, Adult or Child positions. Become familiar with the different qualities of these positions so that you can recognize them quickly – then you will be able to react to them appropriately.

What position is best for you?

Your Child position is the lowest position of all and brings out your girlfriend's Adult and Parent, both of which will be on your back. But your Child is a valuable source of humor, laughter, energy and vitality.

In logical Adult you will struggle with her unpredictable world of 'emotional intelligence' and she will constantly wrong foot you. In Parent she will cut across your logic with her 'superior' opinions. But your Adult is important for personal boundary setting and establishing the rules of the relationship.

If you want to be one up, you operate from the 'superior' position of Parent. There is no 'one up' from Parent. But what aspect of Parent is best? Disciplinarian? Authoritarian? Protector? Rescuer? Father? Teacher? You don't want to end up being a horribly arrogant, rude lecturer.

Integration: Using Parent to control your Child

You have to learn to integrate Parent, Adult and Child.

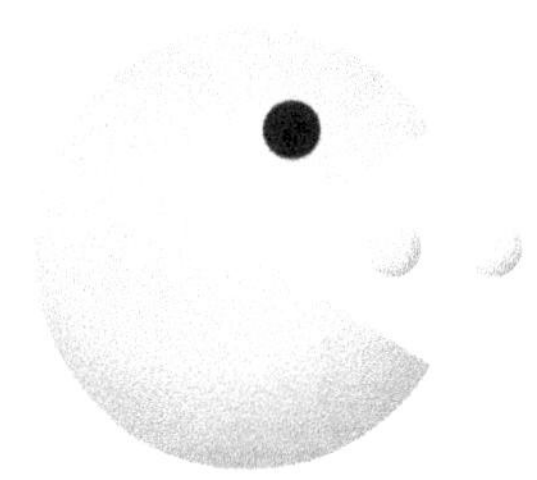

Remember – you are PAC-man. This means that you function mainly in Parent to stay one up, but you make use of your Child. You don't completely ignore your Child or else you will become boring, humorless and arrogant. Your Child provides you with mischief, humor, laughter, energy, vitality and passion. But if you give your Child total freedom, you will end up being silly, childish, stupid, needy, dependent and an embarrassment to others. You end up acting like a little boy instead of a man and put yourself one down.

An integrated male acts appropriately. He does not function in Child at work or college, **or in his relationships with females**. If you stay in Child she may laugh for a while but will soon get tired or irritated by your immaturity. You are not a 'toy boy". This is another 'put down' used by females to keep males one down. It may sound flattering, but if you step out of line a girlfriend in Parent will soon take control of you. You are not a 'boy' – at worst you are a mature male and at best a man.

So your Child has to be kept on a on a tight leash by your Parent and Adult positions that are best placed to know when and how much to let your Child out, or even to refuse to give it any expression at all. When you do this your playful humor is mature, regulated and appropriate.

So you function in Parent, with sensible, rational Adult close at hand, and in this way you have a constant, masterful authority and you can best decide if, when and how to tap into your Child vitality, vibrancy and energy *as a man*. But your Child does not take over – you don't descend into immature silliness. In a similar way, from your masterful position you decide if, when and how to use your passion [Child] at the right moment, to have a maximum effect on your girlfriend.

Cultivating humor

> **You can get away with the most outrageous insults if you give them with a smile**

Your male pride wants to boast about your self-importance, abilities, sexual skills and attractiveness, and in addition, your Parent position can end up being 'superior', pompous and authoritarian. So if you are best orientated in Parent, how can you minimize this rude, conceited aspect of your Parent so that you are more likeable to others, especially females?

A great tactic is to use self-mockery. To mix self-confidence and humor you once again integrate Parent and Child. In Parent you control the humor of your Child so that it emerges in an appropriate way, and this mischievous humor 'softens' your Parent, creating wry humor. Not laugh-out-loud slapstick humor that belongs to the very young Child, nor the humor of teenagers becoming aware that they have a dick and that girls have breasts – college humor full of sexual innuendo or crude sexual references thinking that crude is funny. Nor do you want to be bitterly sarcastic like females in Critical Parent, because you will insult and belittle your girlfriend. These are not the kinds of humor that you want to display with girlfriends. **You are not a clown**.

Instead you combine 'superior', knowing Parent with the humor, lightness and mischief of Child and you apply this 'knowing humor' to **yourself** as well as to others. You direct it at yourself to deflate your own pride. If you are always boasting, you will not be attractive and people will try to take you down a peg or two. But if you use humor on yourself, if your girlfriend tries to 'take you down a peg or two' she will fail because you either

Have already done it for her, or

Simply agree with her [Fogging]

Here is what I mean. Perhaps you have made the mistake of boasting about how many girlfriends you have had:

F: 'You are nothing but a womanizer!' [Critical Parent]

M: 'Correct. I am. I love going out with different girls!' [Parent] Delivered with a broad smile.

Or:

> F: 'You just can't keep a girlfriend can you? Every girl you go out with ends up leaving you!' [Critical Parent using emotive arguments]

> M: 'That's right! - There are so many girls out there and not one of them seems able to keep me.' [Parent] Delivered with an air of humorous despair at having to deal with such a problem.

Or:

> F: 'No!! I am not forgiving you this time! You have gone too far!' [Indignant Child]

You mockingly put your hand on your heart, lower your head, close your eyes and say:

> M: 'My heart is crushed!' Then, with your head still lowered, you look at her still keeping one eye closed. [Parent]

> F: 'Don't you laugh at me!' [Indignant Child or Parent]

> M: 'You are right! I will find a girlfriend who has a better sense of humor!' [Withdrawal Strategy] You then leave. [Parent]

You can deal with compliments in the same way:

> F: 'You are a real gentleman!'

> M: 'If you could see into my mind you would know that I am no gentleman!' [Parent] Delivered with a wry smile.

This humor involves the sarcastic use of words to suggest the opposite of what they normally mean, characterized by mockery, derision, disdain and cynicism - especially self-mockery and self-derision. Females in Critical Parent deliver this humor with sneering malice. But you want to get your girlfriend in bed – not give her a verbal roasting! So you mix your sarcasm or derision with your most charming smile and an ability to laugh regularly and heartily at almost anything - **especially at the world and its problems**, with an easy, relaxed charm, carefree lightness of humor and laughter that also has a sense of 'superior' Parental indulgence.

Not being childish is essential. Your Parent and Adult regulate your humor so that it is witty, intelligent and appropriate. Your Child is your source of fun, laughter and mischief feeding the humor that enables you to 'get away' with all kinds of 'put downs' and criticisms, so that people are amused at the very insults that you direct at them.

If your humor is missing, your comments turn into harsh insults and offensive, destructive criticism

Integration: Harnessing your Adult

Whilst in Parent you make use of your Adult as well, as appropriate. Work and careers are about reliability, punctuality, honesty, straightforwardness and so on, so if you are to be successful at work, you act from Adult.

*If your girlfriend is in Adult, you respond by moving to **your** Adult to treat her with honesty, respect and straightforwardness.*

When you relate to females:

Females in Adult are the only exception

to you being in Parent

So you don't ignore your Adult. When it comes to making decisions, setting boundaries, and structuring your relationship, your Adult is the most logical, analytical, honest, respectful and straightforward position to be in. You also need to access your Adult to analyse and evaluate how to respond appropriately to your girlfriend, based on her own orientation.

The integrated male

So, as PAC-man you function mainly in Parent but pay attention all the time to your Adult as well as your Child.

With the exception of females who are in their Adult position

You function in Parent position

You have to be in Parent to counter any female self-proclaimed Parent 'superiority', and when Girlfriends are in Child you **still** have to be in Parent because your rational Adult will not usually succeed in countering her emotional tactics.

In Parent

You are fully in control of what you do - *or don't do*

If she acts or speaks in an unacceptable way you quickly evaluate the situation [Adult] and change to Critical, Authoritarian or Disciplinarian Parent.

What happens to naughty children? They are put on the 'naughty step'.

In addition, you can appropriately access your Child at any time as a source of your humor, energy, laughter and mischief – using these qualities to hold back the harshness of or any bitterness in your sarcastic Parent. You become a charming rogue. A scoundrel, playfully mischievous [Child] with an air of superiority [Parent]. You have a *hint* of being immoral – not held back by rules [Child]. You wear smart clothes [Adult] and are very much your own person, setting your own course – and are not blown off course by other people – especially females [Parent].

O.K. This may seem new, strange and even difficult – but it isn't. To help you, I will give lots of examples so that you can see what I mean *and* have some tactics to try for yourself.

Dealing with a girlfriend in her Child

With a girlfriend in Child you operate in Parent without fail. You are wise to all her emotional ploys and you are NOT a victim of them, but as Parent, you find her *acceptable* Child behavior amusing *unless:*

    a) Her behavior or attitude crosses your boundary, or

    b) She moves to Adult.

If she moves to Adult, you also immediately move to Adult

But if her Childish behavior or attitude continues to be unacceptable, you withdraw your humor [Withdrawal Deterrent] and allow your authoritarian Critical Parent to come to the fore. The sparkle in your eye disappears; your smiles and laughter vanish and are replaced by stern seriousness. You don't move to Adult and try to reason with her because while she is in Child she is emotionally irrational.

Both males and females who are in Child sometimes unconvincingly try to make out that they are an Adult capable of making their own independent decisions and they say that they should be treated as such. If your girlfriend is in Child but trying to make out that she is an independent Adult, you *sarcastically* treat her as an Adult, [Parent using Child humor] until *you* are convinced [Adult] that she has *genuinely* moved to her rational Adult position.

For example - you ask her 'permission' to sit down using an exaggerated tone of voice, making a point of bowing to her - 'May I sit down?' ***but then you sit down anyway before she can answer.*** In this kind of approach you make exaggerated gestures – a big show of opening a door for her, bowing very low as she goes through the door and so on, and use an element of mockery – 'After **you** miss!'. You aim to puncture her inflated Child vanity. ***The fact that she has to <u>ask</u> to be treated like an Adult gives away the fact that she is not in Adult.*** Genuine Adult positions bring about respect, trust and common sense in other people as a natural response.

In Child she will have **emotional** aims: 'I want him.' Then her 'logical' schemes follow on from this [Emotional Intelligence], as she tries to get who or what she wants. For example, she may feel: 'I want him but he's not giving me any attention. I'll get the attention of all the other males by flirting with them then he will notice me'. She then uses the 'other males' shamelessly and they don't usually see her tactics because they are too busy being flattered by her 'attention' [Male Child]. Her plan is: 'When he sees me getting attention he will feel excluded from the group and need to join it'. She takes her own need to belong [Child] and wrongly assumes that males have the same needs.

If your girlfriend adopts the position of Child 'little princess', seeing herself as the most special female in the room, she will be amazed if males don't try to kiss her [Child Vanity]. If she asks you to kiss her, you can reply:

> M: 'I think I'll wait for you to grow up.' [Parent using Child humor to puncture female Child vanity]

Or

> M: 'I don't kiss children.' [Parent using Child humor to puncture female Child vanity]

If at some point you do decide to kiss her and then as you move forward to kiss her on her lips she offers her hand, cheek or her forehead instead, pull back and refuse to kiss her saying:

> M: 'I'll wait for better things to come along.' [Parent using Child humor to puncture female Parent 'superiority']

She is either trying to set your agenda or being childishly pretentious, but your response is the same – you refuse to kiss her at all and maintain control of yourself and the situation.

She may seem vibrant, energetic, playful and a risk-taker – she may want to kiss you (or more) in situations where both of you might be discovered. Such qualities make her very attractive, but she may only be looking for another new experience or relationship. She may openly flirt with other males in front of you, constantly entering into brief, new relationships, but soon becoming bored, dropping her new male friend like a stone to move on to the next one, with little sense of the emotional pain she causes. An older male may give up his marriage and home for her, only to find that she quickly finds him boring and irritating, and never thought of their relationship as permanent. Despite his anger she will walk out just the same.

In her 'Little Princess' Child she is often willful, stubborn and self-opinionated and may try to order people about - but in the same way that a child tries to tell adults what to do.

Remember:

> **Always respond to females in their**
>
> **Child by being in your Parent**

Here is an example:

You are both going to a party where there will be a mixture of people of all ages. She deliberately picks an outrageous, shocking or unconventional dress to wear at the party [Child]. You don't approve because, [Male Adult], she is with you and many of your friends at the party will disapprove of how she dresses and even be offended – seeing her as 'common trash'. But it is no use *reasoning* with her so you adopt your Parent and say:

> M: 'You're not wearing that! You'll wear a different dress tomorrow when I call to take you to the party or we'll stay at home all night.' [Critical Parent, Personal Boundary Setting, Threat of Withdrawal Deterrent]

She pretends to agree but deceitfully plans to wear the dress anyway [Child], planning to wear her dress and go to the party before you arrive to pick her up. But her plans go wrong – her transport does not arrive - so when you call at her house she's wearing the dress that you were critical of. You repeat your deterrent:

> M: 'I told you to wear a different dress or we stay at home.' [Critical Parent, Personal Boundary Setting, Threat of Withdrawal Deterrent]

At this point you are still one up.

> F: 'Oh? Afraid you might have to stand up and defend me? Are you scared?' [Child, Diversion into Emotional Trap, Male Vanity Trap]

You fall into her trap – you are not scared and will not be accused of such – so, feeling angry [Child], you take her to the party with her wearing her dress. You are now one down.

People at the party stare at her, give disapproving looks and some walk away rather than be seen talking to her. She *feels* uncomfortable and excluded and quite soon she wants you to take her home to rescue her from her discomfort.

You regain your position of being one up by refusing to take her home [Parent]. More than that, you insist on continually meeting other people as you hold on to her and she clings firmly by your side feeling more and more uncomfortable. Then you insist that she dances with you. When others leave the dance floor making her feel exposed, you dance around the floor with her for all to see [Critical Male Parent].

If your girlfriend gets her own way by scheming against your stated wishes, if she feels any discomfort, be aware of it and **refuse to let her avoid it**. Make her face the consequences of her choices, withdrawing your support, humor, and your role as rescuer/protector. You may even aggravate her discomfort (She wanted it – She got it!).

In this example, her Child behavior is unacceptable enough for you to finish the relationship. At the end of the evening you take her to her front door, (with her parents) and you say to her mother:

> M: 'Goodnight Mrs. Jones'. [Male Adult – polite and respectful]

Then to her you say:

> M: 'Goodbye Susan' [Male Parent – cold, formal and humorless]
>
> F: 'Oh? Have you made up your mind to finish with me?' [Female Child]
>
> M: 'No. *You* have made up my mind for me'. [Male Parent]

You leave and don't contact her again [Withdrawal Deterrent].

Still in her Child she may be convinced that you will come

running back to her that very evening:

> F: 'He'll come back. When he does, tell him I've gone to sleep and I'll see him tomorrow.' [Female Child]

But you don't go back

A girlfriend in Child orientation will expect and demand your full attention. Your job, hobbies and friendships have to take second place - especially any friendships you have with other females – such friendships will make her jealous. If she sees you with another female she will start an Inquisition:

> F: 'Where did you meet her?' [Angry Child]

> M: 'She's an old friend.' [Adult]

> F: 'Obviously. Did you play hopscotch with her in the nursery playground?' [Move to Critical Parent]

> M: 'She was at University with me.' [Adult]

> F: 'You must have a great deal in common. Invite me the next time you meet up to work together.' [Disdainful Parent]

> M: 'I will.' You walk away. [Parent - said without humor and as a **threat**. Withdrawal Deterrent]

She will demand your time:

F: 'Why didn't you call me?' [Angry Child]

M: 'I didn't want to.' [Adult]

F: 'Thanks! That's nice!' [Move to Critical Parent]

M: 'I wanted time to think.' [Adult]

F: 'How convenient! Men always want the convenience and none of the difficulties. What did you think about? Your job?' [Critical Parent]

M: 'I thought about us.' [Adult]

F: 'You don't expect me to believe that do you?' [Critical Parent]

M: '**I don't care** what you believe!' [Critical Parent and Detachment – willingness to walk away]

F: 'I ought to slap your face!' [Critical Parent Last resort to violence]

M: 'Why don't you try it?' [Parent – cool, threatening tone of voice, possibly moving forward]

Teenagers take heed.

Don't hand out sweeties to her when what she needs is the sharp bite of your indifference. '**I don't care**' will make her thirst like a mouthful of hot peppers.

When she leans very close and you feel her breast pressing against your body – give her no reaction – don't move, not even your eyes. Act as if nothing has happened.

Dealing with a girlfriend in her Parent

If your girlfriend is in her Parent position then you must be in your Parent too so as to remain at least on an equal footing with her.

> ## Refuse to allow her any 'superiority' at all

Deal with her attempts to tell you what you 'should', 'ought' and 'must' do by using your own Parental 'superiority', mixed with humor [Child] - at least to start with. If she continues in Critical or Nurturing Parent then you relate to her with a more authoritarian Critical Parent approach. You don't tolerate her attitude and dismiss her comments with contempt by using a critical tone of voice or a disbelieving tone of voice.

> ## *Never* move to Child or Adult in this situation –
>
> ## it will put you one down

Here is the difference between her Adult and Parent positions:

F: 'We need to talk' [Parent] (Commanding tones)

As opposed to:

F: 'I think it would be useful if I could talk with you. Could we do that?' [Adult]

When your girlfriend is in her Parent position, her bitter, or malicious sarcasm comes to the fore. You can respond to her sarcastically by being formal and using her surname –

> M: 'So, *Mrs. Smith*, what have you to say about...' (Done with a charming smile) [Parent with Humor].

You use 'Parental formality' with humor to begin with. You say her surname using slight exaggeration – mock seriousness that tells her that her tactics don't fool you.

Brush aside her Critical Parent comments with humor. For example, if she catches you listening in to other people's conversations and then tries to tell you off, simply reply:

> M: 'I've learned a lot of valuable information this way' and then laugh. [Parent with humor]

Use mock facial expressions of disbelief when she speaks to you in this Parental way, or give the mocking impression that you are offended, or disappointed in her because she has taken such an attitude.

On the other hand you could increase your own self-confident Parent position and become louder, appear more confident, interrupting her conversation.

You can bring her down to Adult by asking her to give reasons. If she *does* move to Adult then **in this case** you stay in Parent to get and stay 'one-up'.

Here is an example – a female at work says:

> F: 'I hear you've got a new lady friend. You must bring her here so that we can give her our approval.' [Parent]

> M: 'Why on *earth* would I need your approval?' [Spoken in Parent tones of disbelief requesting Adult justification from the female]

Or:

> M: 'Who has put you in charge of vetting who I go out with?' [Spoken in Parent tones of disbelief requesting Adult justification from the female]

> F: 'I thought you might say something like that' [backing down to Adult and spoken in tones of ironic humor]

Females in their Parent position often question male suffering, discomfort or pain and dismiss it as an over exaggeration or 'con trick', or they flatly contradict and deny its very existence:

> M: 'Ow! That hurt!'

> F: 'Rubbish! It doesn't hurt at all!' [Critical Parent]

She may dismiss your pain by comparing it with her own:

M: 'Ow! That hurt!'

F: 'Rubbish! It doesn't hurt at all! You should give birth to a baby! That hurts!' [Critical Parent]

This is the female 'Giving-birth-martyr' syndrome.

Every time she mentions childbirth

Pain - dismiss it

M: 'Oh no! Not the birth pain syndrome *again*!' [Parent with humor]

She may suggest that males have a lower pain threshold than females. Whether true or not it makes no difference - you flatly deny the believability of such suggestions and if she insists on saying it is true, you ask for evidence –

M: Who says so? What are *your* medical qualifications? Where's the report? How do you know that this is the case? [Parent asking for Adult justification from her]

If she can't provide solid evidence, you have the advantage:

M: 'Exactly! It's just something you made up!' [Parent with humor].

Girlfriends in 'Parent' will act like your mother, trying to set your agenda and telling you off when you do or say things she doesn't like.

But most females have a fear of turning into their *own* mother and sometimes catch themselves: 'Oh no! I sound like my mother!' When you catch her in her Critical Parent, you can say things like:

M: 'Yes mother!' [Parent mocking obedient Child]

Or:

M: 'O.K. Mum'. [Parent mocking obedient Child]

Or you can call her by her actual mother's name:

M: 'Yes Ivy! Er I mean mother!' [Parent mocking obedient Child]

She will try to choose your clothes for you so that you are dressed the way that she wants you to dress.

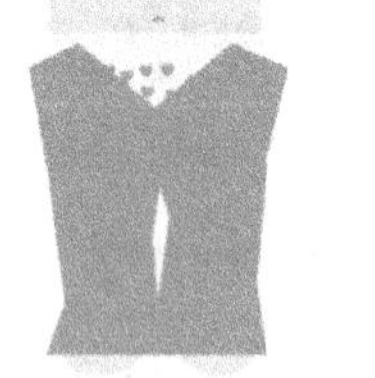

It *is* O.K. to take your girlfriend with you to get her opinion on the clothes you are thinking of buying:

M: 'I'm going to London to buy some clothes. Are you coming?' [Parent/Adult]

You can listen to her opinion and then decide for yourself whether or not to take her advice. But if you allow her to stay in her Parent, she will put herself in command, placing you into 'Child being dressed by his mom'. Resist this as soon as you spot it.

Females never – *ever* – make decisions for you

She can decide which hand she wants to hold her fork in when she has a meal, but she can't be allowed to tell you what, when or how to eat. A strong male knows his own mind – *he* is in control and makes his own decisions. She can give her *opinion* – Hell! Everyone is entitled to an opinion – but he decides whether he will take any notice of it or not.

> F: 'I have a reputation for knowing good clothes. No. Not that one. Take the dark one.' [Parent]

> M: 'You mean this?' [Pointing to an item of clothing]. [Adult]

> F: 'Yes' She may then give 'superior' reasons as to why you should go with her choice. [Parent]

> M: 'I wouldn't know. I only just have time to get dressed in the morning. I like the striped suit better.' [Here you move to *emotive* language – to your *emotional* preference – something she can't argue with].

> F: 'You can be very obstinate' [Critical Parent]

> M: 'I began when I was young.' [Parent with Child humor]

Sometimes females in their Parent position express a 'superior', dismissive disinterest. She stays near you but seems more interested in herself – adjusting her hair, glancing at herself in a mirror and so on - showing an attitude of contempt as though you have just fell out of the back of a dog's arse.

You can show her that you have noticed her attitude but **don't care**. You can also use certain one-liners in a dry, deadpan style, to good effect. This is clever, witty, sharp and quick – not all males have such skills. If you think you do have such qualities, here are some starters:

'Every time I look at you I get a strong desire to be on my own!'

'You can leave any time you like you know.'

'What's the matter? Are you too shy to tell me that you detest me?' [Parent with humor]

She may respond in a tone of voice that suggests that you a are a piece of shit that she has accidentally stepped in:

F: 'Have we met?' [Parent - said with disdain]

M: 'I've never seen you before and enjoyed every moment of it.' [Parent – with Child humor]

Or:

F: 'I've seen you somewhere....'

M: 'Do you use public transport?'

F: 'No.'

> M: 'You probably don't recognise me with my clothes on. I pose for the male underwear advertisements.' [Parent with Child humor]

If she walks away, still superior and disinterested, you can try:

> M: 'Hey! You just spoiled the beginning of a horrible relationship!' [Parent – with Child humor]

Dealing with a female in her Adult

Females in their Adult position are closest to your male viewpoint – thinking, evaluating and reasoning. You withdraw your humor *as a courtesy* and take her seriously treating her with respect. In almost every situation, if she moves to her Adult position, you immediately do the same and respond to her in a straightforward, respectful way, with good manners so that both of you are in common sense Adult. No power game is played here and you have no hidden agenda to try to be one up.

If she says she can take care of herself, (in Adult), you let her. She is saying she does not need a 'Parent' to look after her. You can give her compliments, such as kissing her hand in greeting. You speak honestly and directly to her and may even speak bluntly - including giving critical evaluations of her or her actions, but there is no deceit and no covering up of your own failings either. An Adult-to-Adult relationship is business-like - but you are prepared to use deterrents if she breaks her word.

If your girlfriend is mainly in Adult you may give her a lavish monetary allowance for clothes, jewelry, food or housekeeping, giving her charge over the home budget for example - *but you will also tell her that you will carefully check the account books from time to time*. If she complains you will point out:

> M: 'You would do the same if it was the other way around!' [Adult]

The integrated male in default Parent position

As an integrated male (PAC-man), you keep female friends as long as they amuse you. You show no *respect* for females in their Child or Parent positions, and you certainly have no fear of them. You are self-assured and you have learned to look boldly and directly at a female - giving her a cool, 'superior' look, weighing her up as if you know what she looks like naked **but you don't look lustfully and leeringly at her [Child].**

You don't *obviously* chase after females because if you do, you put yourself at a disadvantage. You don't ask for a photo of her, beg to see her, beg to hold her hand or to have a kiss [Child]. You calculate ways [Adult] to see her under the cover of other business, or to 'accidentally' bump into her in town and so on. You wait for her response of showing interest in  you. If she asks for some kind of help, you may offer to help her as part of a straightforward deal if you think that

> You will gain financially or

> Get an opportunity to see her more often.

If she breaks her word you will hold her accountable [Adult].

You see through her Childish games and laugh at them as well as her Parental criticism. You act as though you are older and wiser, taking the lead. You refer to her by using 'pet names' such as 'Good girl', 'My dear', 'Baby', 'Babe', 'Babes', 'Honey', 'Darling', 'Young lady', 'Sugar', 'My pet' or 'My pretty' in condescending, sarcastic ways but always with humor. If she objects you still call her 'Babe' and say something like:

> M: 'No, I'll call you Babe. I'll probably forget your name later - 'Babe' is easier to remember!' [Parent with humor]

You seek to build up her passion [Child] but then leave just as she is expecting a kiss. [Puncturing of Female Child vanity]. She may reply:

> F: 'I hope you don't come back!' [Angry Disappointed Child]

> M: 'Oh but I will!' [With a smile and twinkle in your eye. Parent with humor]

In this way her passion is left to simmer and build up over time, and you have shown her that it is *you* who decides if and when you will return, not her.

Betrayal

If she betrays you, you will be angry and may even be physically rough – but not violent. As authoritarian, disciplinarian, punishing Parent you make her face  up to the consequences of her actions in front of others, and withdraw your role as her protector and rescuer, making her face her accusers alone. Your sharp tongue will no longer be softened by mocking humor, smiles or laughter. You will not let her avoid her betrayal or its consequences and you will talk about it whether she wants to or not - [Parent].

F: 'Please...' [Child]

M: 'I *don't* please!' [Parent]

F: 'I *won't* listen!' [Child]

M: 'You *will* listen!' [Parent]

There may be a threat -

M: 'If you get out of that chair once more...' [Parent]

You will no longer be interested in her Childish explanations or excuses. As far as you are concerned, there *is* no excuse for such betrayal and you will tell her exactly what is going to happen and she will have little or no say in it. [Parent]

Rewards and Punishments

You encourage your girlfriend's desirable behaviors by giving her rewards, and you discourage her undesirable behaviors by either failing to reward such behavior or by giving some kind of punishment. But 'punishment' is too strong, so I use the milder word 'deterrent' - something that discourages or deters her undesirable behavior or attitude. Here is the principle:

Her desirable behavior earns rewards

Her undesirable behavior earns deterrents

A 'deterrent' is a penalty that must **always** closely follow her undesirable behavior. If she shows undesirable behavior today, you don't carry out your deterrent next week. There has to be a strong link in *her* mind between what you consider to be her undesirable behavior or attitude and the deterrent that inevitably follows on from it.

> # Deterrents are applied <u>immediately</u> after her unacceptable behavior occurs

Here is another important rule:

> **Don't issue exaggerated threats that**
>
> **you are not prepared to carry out,**
>
> **or are unable to carry out**

Your threat of a deterrent is not a bluff. You are not playing a game. Be ready to have your threat challenged and be ready to use it. If you back down, any threats you make in the future will be meaningless and have no effect.

Defining unacceptable behavior

What exactly is unacceptable behavior? First, you have to realize that being in your Parent position does not mean that you always act like a dictator so that you always get your own way and she has to do as she is told. Not at all – you want her to be independent, reach her potential, follow her interests and ambitions and have a circle of friends of her own – male or female, and of course, to take responsibility for the decisions and choices that she makes. Some of this involves negotiated compromises (Adult) on both sides.

Her behaviour becomes unacceptable when she seeks to take away these very same qualities from you. It is unacceptable for her to:

Make unasked for decisions for you

Be sarcastic, critical or dismissive about you in front of others

'Organize' you without you being asked

Give you orders, commands or 'instructions' about what you 'should', 'ought' or 'must' be doing

Ignore and go against what you have arranged together

Blame you for her mistakes or failures

Act as if she is your 'superior'

Play the 'emotional card' to get what she wants

Try and stop you having female friends

Try to stop you going out with your mates once a week

Try to stop you from engaging in your interests and

hobbies

Diminish your self-control

Treat you as immature, inadequate, ineffective or useless

These are just some of the things that your girlfriend may try to do that are unacceptable behaviors. But the core arrangement is this: You don't tell her how to live her life and in the same way, you don't expect her to invade and organize your life. Such boundary crossing has to be mutually negotiated and agreed upon in Adult. Once you have told her that her behavior is unacceptable

> If she continues to behave unacceptably it always results in you immediately and calmly applying your deterrent in a determined way

There is no backing down and no inconsistency in your use of deterrents. She has to be in no doubt whatsoever that you mean what you say. You have to be focused and committed to this principle so that she feels that there is an inevitable link between her unacceptable behavior and you putting a deterrent in place.

The plain fact is that if your girlfriend is *habitually* and *persistently* in her Parent or Child, she probably will not change despite your encouragement to do so – this is her personality and character – it may change over a considerable period of time or as a result of dramatic life experiences, but although you may well use the approaches outlined in the next chapters, she may not learn to change. If you see this resolute firmness in her behavior, she is failing to learn from your use of these approaches and if this is the case, you may well eventually consider that the relationship takes too much of your effort because she is not learning. You have to ask – is this what you want for the rest of your life?

4 SELF CONFIDENCE

Your girlfriend wants to put herself on top or may feel that she is already one up. All of her talk about 'equality' is a distraction as she seizes the upper hand. But if you are one down it is not a permanent defeat - with effort and learning you can recover.

So remember these principles:

> ## If you are not one up, you are one down

> ## NEVER talk openly to her about being 'one up'

No. You constantly **think** and tell yourself **in your head** that you are one up and in charge of yourself and your decisions.

There are some essential rules that you don't tell your girlfriend – these make up your **hidden** inner position. Her emotional base is 85% hidden below the surface, so some principles of your position are hidden in the same way.

Operate from self-confidence

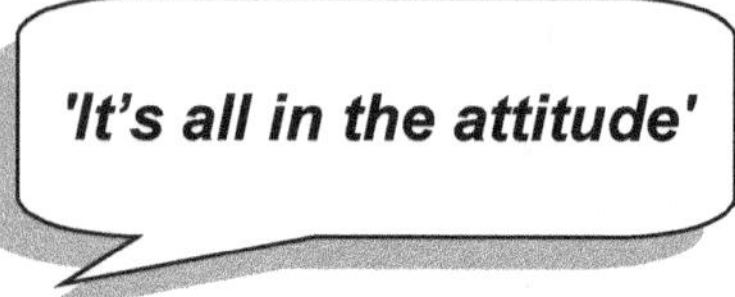

Always relate to females with self-confidence from the start:

> M: 'I couldn't help noticing that you are the prettiest girl I've seen. I think you should give *me* some attention.' [Parent]

It's never too late for you to develop self-confidence.

Self-confidence comes from within. It is **not dependent on what others think of you or how they evaluate you**. If your self-confidence depends on other people, you lose control of it. You hand it over to other people who are busy defending their *own* self-esteem – which they often do by putting others down a peg or two. Time to grow up. **You** don't need to put other people down to get self-confidence. Value yourself for who you are, regardless of what other people think. You're not perfect - but you're not far off – a Parent attitude.

Cultivating self-confidence

If you have low self-confidence then every setback and rejection will seem much bigger than it really is. Males who are successful with females will tell you they have been rejected many times - the most successful have been rejected more than most - rejection is par for the course. It *will* happen so expect it.

These three confidence-building tactics are great to start with:

Challenge any negative thoughts you make about yourself and contradict them by using positive self-talk

Look to self-confident people who you know and use them as examples for your own attitude and behavior

Read self-help/assertiveness books and carry out the exercises they recommend

Self-confidence and a position of strength

When you have a self-confident attitude you operate from a position of strength, where YOU are the prize that is worth having, the man *she* will be lucky to be with and win.

If previous relationships with females have broken down, remember that they have **failed to keep *you***. They did not succeed in keeping hold of you and failed to keep the relationship going. They lost the prize.

Self-confidence, arrogance and pride

When your girlfriend sees you meeting up with a self-confident male friend they may say:

> F: 'You don't want to be mixing with likes of him!' [Parent]

Your response is:

> M: 'Who are you to tell me who I meet up with?' [Parent spoken in authoritative or incredulous tone of voice]

You make your own choices in life.

Females often class self-confident males as being *arrogant*. But remember, when she is in Critical Parent or Bossy Princess Child, this is exactly what *she* is like, putting on an air of self-importance at your expense.

But let's distinguish between self-confidence, arrogance, pride and vanity.

Arrogance is an **exaggerated** opinion of yourself and your skills.

Pride is an attitude in which you **incorrectly** think that you are better than and superior to other people, especially females.

Vanity is an **excessive** pride in your appearance and your sense of attractiveness to females.

These are not examples self-confidence. Best to abandon arrogance, pride and vanity.

> # If people pay you compliments,
>
> # immediately dismiss them

This seems to be the opposite of what I have been saying earlier but the difference is this –

Inwardly you are self-confident and self-assured and

Outwardly you act and speak in a self-confident and assured way, but

> ## *You don't openly boast about yourself,*
>
> ## *your achievements or talents*

If anyone praises you, you are quick to put yourself down - even though you actually keep your self-confident and assured manner.

You dismiss both criticism *and praise* as irrelevant, brushing them aside with humor, putting you in a position of strength. If anyone calls you a 'gentleman', a 'hero', or a 'lovely man' e.t.c., you brush aside such compliments immediately:

M: 'I am not a [gentleman, hero, lovely man] you know'. [Parent with humor and dark suggestiveness]

You can even add something negative:

> M: 'I am no gentleman. I'm only concerned to make money'. [Parent with humor]

Your Parent position demands self-confidence and *appropriate* pride, but not arrogance or vanity. It demands *regulated* pride:

> F: 'I am convinced that you have no faults. You say so yourself, without trying to hide it.'

> M: 'No, I have plenty of faults'

You don't say this in a shy, embarrassed or uncertain way but in a confident, assured way, that suggests you **don't care** what others think, don't need their praise or fear their criticism. You are confident *in yourself*, but **you don't have an over-inflated opinion** of yourself or your skills or work. You don't praise yourself or boast about your achievements in front of others:

> M: 'I am poorly qualified to recommend myself.'

You definitely don't boast about your sexual prowess, or how attractive you are to females. If you do you set yourself up like a target in a shooting gallery. Instead, you are self-confident and self-assured – so self-assured that you don't need to advertise yourself to others.

Girlfriends will seek to gain an advantage over you by either:

> Putting down your vanity

Or doing the exact opposite and

> Nursing your vanity.

When a girlfriend nurses your vanity, she will keep flattering you but also keep you dangling by not committing to a relationship with you or not making definite arrangements – she is all promise and no delivery.

But males are often so vain that they believe *anything* that females say and do to flatter them.

She may use emotional displays like crying to gain favors, gifts or attention from you, flattering you as her Protector / Rescuer / Provider [Child]. A female may use physical closeness – invasion of your personal space, or false intimacy - putting her head on your shoulder or putting her hand in your pocket 'to keep warm' even though you don't know her that well. She may give you child-like looks, adopt a child-like voice, look helpless or give pleading looks. She may use your Christian name when she doesn't know you that well. She may flatter you with false praise:

> F: 'Oh Mr. Jones...Darren...may I call you Darren? You are so clever Darren and I love a clever man!' [Child as she gets too close to you]

She may flatter you by agreeing that you are always right – but then later ignore you and do her own thing anyway once she has got what she wanted.

Females massage your excessive belief in your own attractiveness to others, especially to females, and inflate your excessive rating of your own skills. But while you are dazzled by your own attractive brilliance, she dupes you into letting her have her own way.

Be wise to these tactics and have no 'proud male vanity' that she can puncture or reinforce, no reputation she can make dirty or praise, no behavior she can encourage you to boast or be guilty about. You **don't care** what others think or say about you, your standing, reputation, character or behavior.

If your girlfriend refuses to forgive you [Child] over something you've done so she can put you down and make you plead for her forgiveness, you mockingly put your hand on your heart and declare sarcastically:

M: 'Another hope crushed!' [Parent with humor]

You don't need her forgiveness and **don't care** whether she has a high opinion of you or not.

She may try to make you feel guilty and drag you into the darkness of the emotional realm. You can express a complete lack of guilt or an untroubled conscience:

> M: 'I sleep easy at night.' [Parent]

As you dismiss your own self-reputation, you are equally mockingly dismissive of female vanity.

For example, you may give your girlfriend a surprise gift. She is pleased with it (because it boosts her Child vanity). You point out that you always expect payment for your gifts and always get paid. You tell her in effect that your gifts are not free - you expect something in return. You also tell her that these gifts are to enhance her feminine charms - *this* is the reason you buy her gifts and you do nothing without reason. If she is still pleased to accept your gift, you may even tell her that you are leading her into a pit that she will fall into.

If she asks what you expect to be paid, you are vague:

> M: 'That remains to be seen!' [Parent]

If she suggests a form of payment herself, such as a kiss on her cheek [Female Child], you tell her outright that she flatters herself. In this way you puncture the balloon of her inflated vanity.

You don't reward her vanity

You do **not** kiss her and do **not** move forward to hug her. If she offers her cheek for you to kiss you say:

> M: 'I know prettier, cleverer, kinder women than you -

but somehow I remember and think of you.' [Parent]

Her Child vanity is punctured again.

She may then say that she doesn't want your gifts. (Because you have punctured her vanity by telling her that you expect to be paid, so she has a Child tantrum) [Unacceptable behavior]. You can either tell her that:

> M: 'I decide whether I bring you presents or not and I will bring you presents as long as it pleases me!' [Parent with male Adult establishing the rules]

Or you can withdraw her gift and say:

> M: 'Then I will take it to a lady who **will** appreciate it!' and you put the gift back in its box and take it with you as you leave, puncturing her vanity again. [Parent and Learning Theory Withdrawal Deterrent].

But if she pleads for it back you give her the gift, with a smile.

Just as you don't boast about yourself, in the same way she is not worth as much as her inflated vanity likes to think. *You* can tell her that she looks pretty, but if *she* says she looks pretty, or that 'she is worth it', you tell her that you know other females who are prettier and more worthy than she is:

> M: 'I've seen prettier women - but you'll do!' [Parent said with a smile and a tone of disdain].

So when I say you operate with self-confidence I don't mean rude, arrogant conceit or excessive pride - I mean an inner attitude of self-assurance, a sound **inner** belief in your own abilities, strong enough for you not to need to broadcast it.

Falling into the 'men are superior' male vanity trap

Females in Parent are good at promoting their own 'superiority' and at putting males into their Child and therefore 'less than useless'.

If you point out that you have done something better than females, you fall into a trap. For example in a team test, the males perform better and quicker. As a result, you may boast:

> M: 'I can't help noticing that the men have performed best.' [Mischievous Parent]

> F: 'That's doubtful - whether you are all men!' [Critical Parent]

You have brought this critical sarcasm on yourself - even if you made the comment in fun. You have brought together a couple of mistakes. You:

> Started a derogatory exchange and

> Fell into the boasting vanity trap

Much better for you to *respond* to females and deflate your *own* vanity if appropriate, as we have just seen.

If you can't resist saying something, much better to use the word **'male'** instead of 'men':

> M: 'I can't help noticing that the males have performed best.' [Mischievous Parent]

This makes it harder for a female to respond, though she may still quickly reply with:

> F: 'That's doubtful - whether you are all men!' [Critical Parent]

You are now in a better position to recover. You can say:

> M: 'I said *males*, not men. I can see why you females perform poorly - you don't pay attention.' [Mischievous Parent]

If she still insists on her comment:

> F: 'It is doubtful whether any of you are males **or** men!' [Critical Parent]

You can now respond with:

> M: 'You take your panties down first and then I'll take my pants down and we'll see who the male is!' [Parent using Child humor and bluff]

It is extremely unlikely that she will follow up on this bluff *but you have to be prepared to take your pants down* **if** she takes her panties down first! She will of course try and get *you* to take *your* pants down first but *you* were first to call the bluff. Her failure to follow through will mean that *she* is one down - and you can point this out to the others.

Taking charge of yourself

I don't take dictation from any woman

- much less the wife!

Know yourself – self-knowledge is self-empowering. When you know who you are, what your goals and interests are, what your principles are and what approaches you use in relating to females, you then have to maintain and defend your personal values from erosion, attack and crossing of boundaries by females – because they will seek to impose, however subtly, their own standards, agendas, timetables and viewpoints on you.

Your personal principles and goals are sacred, but they are not set forever in stone – you change your values as you continue to learn and develop.

> **It is for you alone to change your values and principles - not for females to presume to change them for you**

There is a boundary line within which you are in charge of yourself, make your own decisions and choose your values, goals, agendas and interests. Define these clearly in your own mind – for example, you may affirm to yourself that 'I decide what food I eat, not other people'.

There will be times when you will have to clearly state your position to other people. For example, a female may start to play the emotional card in trying to persuade you to become a vegetarian. You will have to state your personal boundary line clearly and plainly: '**I don't care** if you are upset that I am not a vegetarian – I love meat and will continue to eat it when and if I like'.

You have to firmly defend your boundary line against all pretenders to your throne

This boundary line weaves through every aspect of your life. Within its borders, you are in charge, make your own decisions and answer only to yourself. You don't explain or defend your position to anyone - especially females. This is who you are, and she has to like, love or appreciate you for who you are. Your boundary line is your front line on the battlefield, and immediately behind it you dig your trenches and set up your weapons.

I have to use warfare metaphors here because females often take it upon themselves to assault your boundary line to try to break through it. Sometimes they succeed. Sometimes they use direct attacks; but more often they try to get 'under the wire'.

They make these invasions to change, challenge or undermine your values, interests, hobbies, self-control and identity, so you label these behaviors as 'unacceptable'. By all means listen to her opinions and as a result you may choose to move your boundary line - your values or goals – in the light of what she says, but such decisions are *your* privilege.

If anyone tries to *impose* a movement of your boundary line, such attempts are 'dishonest', 'underhanded', 'propaganda', 'brainwashing', 'thought control', 'manipulation' and so on. You firmly push back all such invasions by clearly stating where your boundary line is positioned:

> M: 'Do you have my television remote control? It's not for you sweetheart!' [Authoritative Parent].

If a female (or anyone else) makes further unasked for crossings or impositions, you put Withdrawal Deterrents in place because of their continued unacceptable failure to recognise your boundary. Your use of withdrawal Deterrents always – **always** – follow such unacceptable behavior once you have clearly stated where your boundary line is.

With regards to females, your Withdrawal Deterrents usually involve the withdrawal of your protection, support, intimacy, humor or physical presence. It can mean your ultimate withdrawal - terminating the relationship if she is too dumb to learn. By defining yourself and successfully repelling invaders you keep your position of being 'one up'. Any failure of your defense, allowing in intruders, will mean that you are one down.

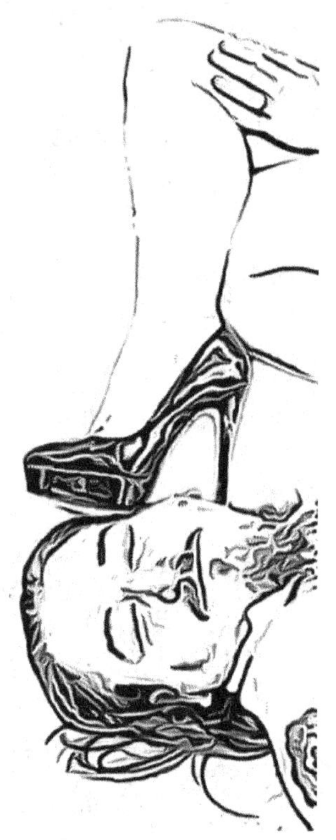

Attempts to *publicly* undermine your self-definition

Girlfriends in Parent sometimes attempt to re-define you *in public*, carrying out Boundary Crossings in situations such as parties, conversations with neighbors, at a business lunch or worse. She imposes unasked for new definitions of who you are that undermine your presentation of yourself.

The giveaway is the tone of her voice. She adopts:

A motherly tone as if talking to a baby; or

A dismissive tone as if you are a piece of shit she has accidentally stepped in.

In both cases, she will *talk about you to other people **as though you are not there***, even though you are right next to her. Since she is in Parent you also have to adopt your Parent position.

For example: When you are with a group of people, as motherly Parent she makes these statements *to* you, or *with* you as though, like a little boy, you agree with her:

> F: 'He loves to have his little extra sleep in the morning!' [Nurturing Parent Mothering spoken in babyish tone of voice]

Or:

> F: 'Oooohh! Who loves his mummy's cooking then?' [Nurturing Parent Mothering spoken in babyish tone of voice]

Alternatively, as Critical Parent she treats you in a derogatory way, as 'a stupid incompetent' or as some sort of 'undesirable foreign species', making her comments a 'superior' tone of voice as a general announcement to anyone within listening distance:

> F: [To others] 'He's done a 'man look' for the coffee. He hasn't really looked at all.'

Then to you and everyone else in aloud voice

> F: 'If I find the coffee in that cupboard you'll be

> wearing it!' [Critical Parent]

Or:

> F: 'Ay up! He's on 'man planet'! Earth calling!' [Critical Parent]

You can adopt a self-determined but carefree approach, as if her comments are like 'water off a duck's back':

> F: 'Look! He's gone into his own world again! He can't find the sugar!' [Critical Parent]

> M: 'Yes mother!' [Parent Humor]

> F: 'Well? Take a closer look!' [Critical Parent]

> M: 'Thanks mother!' [Parent Humor]

> F: 'And don't call me mother!' [Critical Parent]

> M: 'Yes mum. I mean no mum!' [Persistent Parent Humor]

This approach is even more effective if you call her by her mother's Christian name. But you may prefer a more aggressive Parental response:

> F: 'Look! He's in his own world again! He can't find the sugar!' [Critical Parent]

> M: 'Finding the sugar is *your* role. I don't have the time to try and find where *you* have hidden the sugar' [Critical Parent]

> F: 'Well? Take a closer look!' [Critical Parent]

> M: 'No! This kitchen is *your* area! I've got bigger, more important things to think about.' [Critical Parent]

To this you could add, with humor, your own pastimes, interests or jobs –

'I've got a book to write! My ideas might change the world!'

'I've got Trade Union work to sort out, to help the oppressed and victimized!'

'I've got a model railway timetable to run and you are delaying the express!'

Your attitude is that your head is full of much more important and potentially world-changing tasks, causes and decisions than trying to find the sugar.

When it comes to her Nurturing Parent you can try something like this:

F: 'He loves his own special little mug for his cup of coffee' [Female Nurturing Parent – spoken in 'mummy's talking to baby' voice].

M: 'That's right, I like my brew in my favorite cup first thing in the morning and you make quite a good job of providing it - most mornings!' [Male Parent Spoken in schoolmasterly tones. Withdrawal of humor Deterrent]

You can also add:

> M: 'Sometimes it's not warm enough though. You should try a little harder – there's always room for improvement.' [Critical Male Parent Spoken in schoolmasterly tones]. 'That's why us males are here – to help you females to improve' [Critical Male Parent Spoken in 'Daddy's talking to his little girl' voice].

You agree that you like your favorite drink, or extra sleep in the morning, or your mother's cooking [Fogging. See earlier]. But you also make out that there is room for improvement:

> F: 'Oooohh! Who loves his mummy's cooking then?' [Female Nurturing Parent Spoken in 'mummy's talking to baby' voice]

> M: 'My mother's cooking is the best in the world – you've still got some way to go before you reach *her* standard!' [Critical Male Parent Spoken in schoolmasterly tones. Withdrawal of humor Deterrent]

With these sorts of comments be prepared to make your own morning brew, or do your own cooking as she may respond by refusing to do these tasks. Once again, be prepared for your bluff to be called and know in your own mind beforehand just how far you are prepared to go, or to escalate the situation.

General tips about good self-presentation

How you present yourself serves to reflect who you are – your values and standards – so you want to give a good impression. Here are some quick ideas about self-presentation:

Always dress more smartly than your mates.

Always pay attention to colour co-ordination of your clothes.

Always wear well fitting clothes.

Always wear a tie for formal occasions.

Always have good, clean, shiny or polished shoes.

Always check in a full-length mirror to see how the whole package looks.

Always maintain a good posture.

Always go for an understated look where an expensive watch or fancy jacket lining speaks for itself.

Try a formal/casual mode of dress where by simply removing your tie you take away formality resulting in a smart casual, sportsman-like look.

Wear a good after-shave, anti-perspirant and body spray.

Make sure that your teeth are clean and use a mouthwash.

Avoid tattoos - tattoos are O.K. for sailors and army personnel - otherwise avoid them. Men wearing tattoos may think that by having tattoos they are warriors. They aren't.

Avoid earrings, nipple rings and body piercing.

Avoid 'designer stubble' - it usually looks scruffy.

Avoid three quarter length trousers or shorts unless on the beach. If you really must wear them, avoid black socks and black shoes.

Avoid football shirts unless going to a football match.

Avoid 'designer' t-shirts.

Avoid t-shirts with crude, sexist or just silly slogans. Better still, avoid any slogans at all.

Avoid fancy, trendy hairstyles with patterns cut into your hair or such like - especially if you are out of your teens.

Avoid sloppy or unkempt hairstyles.

Avoid cheap or flashy accessories like 'mirror' sunglasses or very large watches.

Avoid wearing clothes that are too young for you - you will look like an ageing juvenile.

Avoid smoking - it was fashionable in the mid twentieth century but not now.

Avoid wearing gym and swimwear that is too small. You don't need budgie-smugglers.

Avoid being smelly, having bad breath or bad teeth.

> **Never – ever – dress down to make your girlfriend feel comfortable**

For example: You are going to a party and she tries to get you to dress 'casually' because she wants to go in jeans and t-shirt. You can decide that she is free to wear what she wants, but you are keeping your self-value and self-presentation at a high level by wearing a suit. If you are the only male wearing a suit at the party, you will get the attention of the females. If she wants to 'dress down' and then feels embarrassed because she is not as smartly dressed as the other females, that is her problem. Ideally of course, you want her to be attractively dressed, because she is an ornament on your arm.

An aside: Females and clothes

You raise standards by dressing smartly and there will be times when you will not find it acceptable for your girlfriend to dress down. But, with the exception of the 'slutty' party dress mentioned earlier, here are two general rules:

> Never criticize the way she is dressed
>
> Never complain about how long
>
> she takes to get ready

You maintain your **own** standards - if you look smarter than she does, she will soon notice and raise her own standards - if she is worth going out with.

Girlfriends often take a long time over their hair, clothes, make up and accessories. But you want her to look and feel good for herself, and sexy for you. So don't complain about how long she takes to get ready - unless you want her to feel untidy, unattractive, uncomfortable and not sexy at all.

Because she wants to *feel* pretty, sexy and attractive, she wants to dress in a way that makes her **feel** this way. This means that she *may want to ignore dress codes,* especially if she is in Child. She may want to go into the Royal Enclosure at Royal Ascot wearing a very short, tight skirt with a low cut top. She says she agrees with the rules but she actually wants to break the rules to satisfy her own emotional needs and be the center of attention.

She will say that she can wear what she wants - what makes her **feel** pretty, attractive, sexy - but the fact is that she can't complain if she then gets unwanted sexual attention and comments from males. As with the example of the unacceptable party dress earlier, you may choose to give her the freedom to dress how she likes - *and take the consequences.* In Child she will not want to take responsibility and when she gets undesirable attention, she will try to make out that it is **your** fault.

The fact is that you don't want her to look like a 'common tart' or wear clothes such as flannelette pajamas after the evening meal, or flip-flops and tracksuit bottoms, or 'onesies' – a single loose-fitting pyjama type 'outfit' that makes her look like a 'snug little bunny' – because she says that they make her feel 'cozy'.

She prefers *this* to sexy black lingerie?

F: 'But it's got a little tail!' [Child attempt at justification]

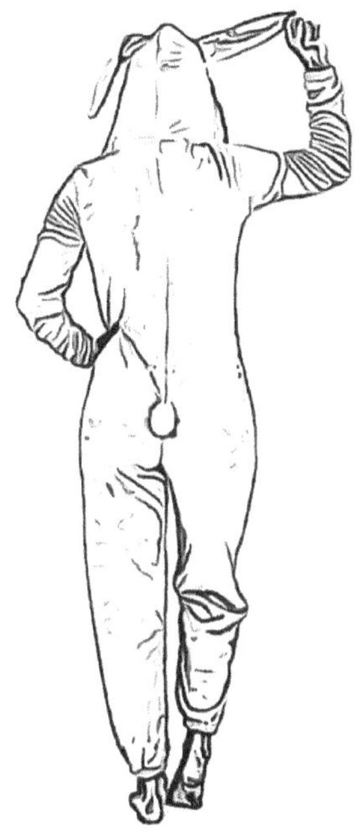

What she thinks of as casual, snug and comfortable is often sloppy laziness revealing a sloppy, slovenly attitude. Ask yourself - would she have worn flip-flops and tracksuit bottoms on her first or second date with you? No? Why should she wear them now? Do you want to take her to bed when she is wearing a 'bunny onesie' instead of sexy lingerie? Remember - *you* are prize worth having. You need to know and define what is acceptable to you.

New relationships: Evaluating her response

You can tell whether a girl is interested in you in thirty seconds to a minute of meeting her. Is there a twinkle in her eye, laughing and giggling and blushing? If you are in company, is she giving you more eye contact than she is to other people? These are all signs that she likes you. If you don't see any of these signs after two minutes at most, move on. Don't waste more of your valuable time. If she isn't clever enough to see that you are a worthwhile prize, she is not worth getting to know.

If you see negative reactions – she looks away or at her watch, or pulls back from you - move on. Don't waste your valuable time no matter how pretty she is.

You **will** be rejected sometimes - everyone gets rejected. But your confidence comes from within you and not from what a particular female, who doesn't even know you, thinks or feels about you. YOU determine how attractive and confident you are. You know more about you than they do. It is up to the girls to catch up - else they will miss out on a great opportunity to be with you.

So, don't waste time trying to get a date with a girl who fails to respond favorably or waste time by wallowing in self-pity if she is not attracted to you. Move on. There's a world of girls out there.

The first date

Where's the best place to go? Not the cinema where you will sit in the dark unable to look at or talk to each other. Not a nightclub - so loud that you will not be able to talk. Better to take her for a quiet but inexpensive meal – but not at your regular local bar where your mates can interrupt. Go to a bar or eatery that is not overly expensive and where you are not known so you can give her your full attention without interruption.

You can make a show of turning off your phone - though you may actually put it into silent mode so if you are contacted by another female you can, at an appropriate moment, go to the men's room and check your calls/messages.

Operate from a position of self-confidence within yourself - a self-confidence that is not dependent on other people. Be self-assured but not arrogant or boastful. Dress to impress, and act masterful and decisive - qualities that females like.

5 OPERATING FROM POWER

'Baby, I don't care!' (Robert Mitchum)

Your greatest power is your power to walk away and say

'I don't care'

If you can't walk away you are weak. You need to be able to walk away from her at any time. Get an independent, self-reliant lifestyle that's not dependent on her - get your own apartment so that you have basic independence, self-determination and are not at her beck and call.

Always have an exit strategy

Walking away is your ultimate Withdrawal Deterrent. Always be aware of where the exits are and have your exit strategy prepared. This means that you:

Never give her your house or car keys

Always have your keys on your person

Then, if you have an argument, you can leave, get in your car, drive to your house and go in without having to ask her for your own keys (which she may choose not to give you).

Your ability to withdraw your self is a potent deterrent and one to develop. For example, if she says she has doubts or concerns about your relationship, you can use this to your advantage:

F: 'I worry that our relationship has started too soon'.

A few days later:

M: 'I've been thinking about what you said and you are right. I don't want to hurt you, but I'm not settled. Like you said, it *is* too soon.'

Always leave before she can accuse you of running away in a crisis - a typical female tactic.

If things aren't going well, best to be up front and talk. You can say that you can see that she is unhappy - her face is miserable all the time and you are not enjoying how the relationship is going either. You can tell her you are going away for a while to think things through and you will see her soon - then you leave - immediately.

If you are upset, depressed or lonely without your girlfriend it will probably only last until you meet another one - there are many females out there who would be lucky to have you as their prize.

After a relationship has finished, she may contact you to ask how you are. She is seeing if:

There is a chance of getting back together

You are lonely, sad, not coping or missing her

You want to try again.

Tread carefully!

If you tell her you want to get back together she may respond with a gloating rejection of you, kicking you while you are down. If you do get back together, you will be in a weak position - always having to be grateful that she 'took you back'. She will have the power and use the threat of finishing the relationship if you don't do what she wants. She will now know that this is a real threat to you because you were unhappy, depressed, and lonely or whatever when you separated.

The recommendation is: don't let her back in. Be polite, say thanks for asking, tell her you are fine and then close the door again. But obviously, circumstances are unique and the decision is up to you.

Sometimes you may have to be firm. A few weeks after a guy had finished a relationship, this text arrived -

F: 'Do we have to go on like this?' [Parent or Adult]

He delayed his reply. [Withdrawal Deterrent] After an hour or so he texted....

M: 'Who is this?'

The suggestion here is that he has deleted her name and number from his contact list. [Withdrawal Deterrent]

F: 'It's Sue. How can you be so cruel?' [Child]

M: No reply. [Withdrawal deterrent]

F: 'Aren't you replying to me?' [Parent, Adult or Child]

It's impossible for him to know her orientation because he can't hear the tone of her voice or see her body language.

> M: No reply. [Withdrawal deterrent]

> F: 'We need to talk.' [Parent or Adult]

His options now include:

> a) No reply, or

> b) Replying after about six hours –

> M: 'We?' or 'Do we?' [Parent Withdrawal Deterrent]

He actually replied:

> M: 'It is too late. Take care.' [Ultimate Withdrawal Deterrent]

When a relationship finishes, or you find yourself in an argument with your girlfriend, she will often use emotional [Child] arguments to drag you into the unfamiliar territory of the emotional swamp.

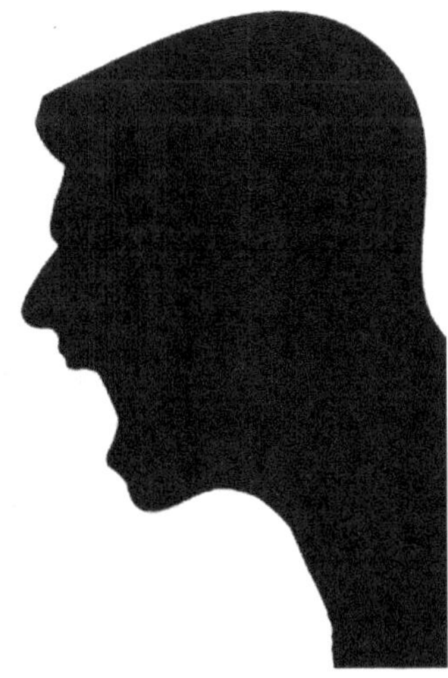

There are no more than six emotional dimensions, but when she feels that her particular emotional approach is not working, (i.e. she is not getting you to do what she wants by being angry), she will switch to another emotional approach to see if that works. (She may start crying). Since there are only five or six approaches she can try, you can often ride them out.

Typical emotional tactics include:

Crying, anguish, fear or panic at having to face life without you. Remember, she got on with life O.K. before she met you - she can get on O.K. with life without you now.

Pleading and self-pity - 'Is it because I am so stupid?' She feels shame, humiliation, embarrassment and guilt and withdraws into herself showing sadness or even depression.

Anger, shouting because she's not got her own way, insulting you, saying she hates you, treating you with contempt and disgust.

Seeing her strong emotions may confuse you and even make you feel threatened, they may throw you off course and shock you because you don't usually live in this emotional sphere or wander into it very often.

One exit strategy is the **'It's out of my control' gambit**. If you have decided to end a relationship, always end your statements with the phrase **'It's out of my control'**, rather like a stylus stuck in a broken vinyl record - keep repeating it:

M: 'I can't go on with this relationship - it's out of my control.'

F: 'We can work it out, together.'

M: 'No, I can't work this out - it's out of my control.'

F: 'But together we can sort out any problems.'

M: 'This problem is too big for me - too big for *us* - it's out of my control.'

F: 'Is there someone else?'

M: 'My emotions are being pulled this way and that -

it's out of my control.'

F: 'There *is* someone else!'

M: I am too weak - the temptation is too great - it's out of my control.'

F: 'You bastard!'

M: 'My passions are too deep - it's out of my control'

F: 'Stop saying it's out of your control!'

M: 'Who can contain the heart? It's out of my control.'

e.t.c.

Degrees of withdrawal

Completely withdrawing yourself is your ultimate Withdrawal Deterrent and it ends the relationship. But there are degrees of withdrawal and different aspects of yourself that you can withdraw.

If she does not appreciate a gift you have bought, withdraw it.

You can withdraw your humor and appear detached and cold.

You can withdraw your approval or interest in what she is doing.

You can be slow to respond to text messages, or not respond at all.

If you normally add kisses or smiley faces to your texts, you can stop.

If you usually send 'good morning' texts or phone her every day, you can stop.

It helps if you establish demonstrations of warmth - they don't take much effort. Once established, they are important things that you can then *stop* doing – effective Withdrawal Deterrents that equally take little effort – in fact the effect will be much larger than your effort.

You can *temporarily* withdraw yourself - put on your coat and leave saying you will see her 'later', or 'tomorrow'. Or you can withdraw to your own room, or to the bar or wherever.

Exit strategies involve some level of withdrawal of the privileges and intimacy that you give her when she is well behaved. This withdrawal happens when she displays unacceptable behavior, or an unacceptable attitude.

> ## The aim of using Withdrawal Deterrents
>
> ## is to get her to change
>
> ## her unacceptable attitude or behavior

But she may not change

Your deterrents may bring the situation to a head - she may not run after you or change her behavior but instead, *she* may threaten *you* –

F: 'If you walk out now we're finished!' [Parent/Adult]

As always,

a) Know your own mind, and

b) Do not make any threat of withdrawal that you are not prepared to carry out.

You decide [Adult] whether the relationship is finished or not and act accordingly. Always assume that she isn't bluffing and *will* carry out her threat. If you back down you risk moving to being one down.

One option is to wait until you are both in Adult position when you can both discuss the matter and move to a negotiated compromise.

If you walk out and she carries through her threat - *she has failed to keep you.*

Failure to use the Withdrawal Deterrent

If for any reason you feel unable to use your Withdrawal Deterrent then you are one down and at her beck and call. You have lost your power.

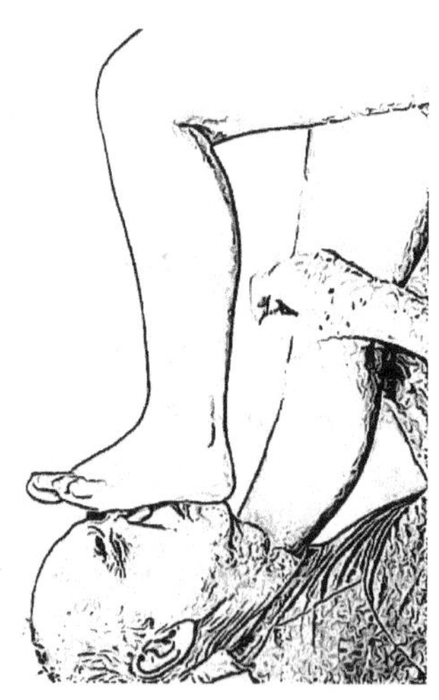

You have to be able to walk away yourself or let her walk out of your life if you want to maintain control of yourself.

It is no use letting her to walk away and then, within a day or two, sending her a stream of texts or phone calls.

You may think that some degree of compromise is necessary to maintain the relationship. For example, you may think that 'keeping the peace' is a good reason to compromise. But there is a boundary line drawn in the sand, a perimeter fence – don't allow her to cross it without your permission.

You build your 'perimeter fence' complete with alarm bells, and then patrol it and maintain your personal, private space to keep control over your own life and agenda.

I want to make this clear –

> ***When you make compromises, you move your boundary line to a position defined by your girlfriend***

When you let her have her way, you allow her to decide where your perimeter fence is located.

She may give you ultimatums, threats or have emotional tantrums because you are not compromising and letting her do what she wants. When uses these kinds of tactics:

She is using a Withdrawal Deterrent on you

In effect she is saying:

If you don't compromise, if you don't do what I want, then I will pull away from you, or even finish with you completely

If **you** are unable to walk away, you let her move your boundary line to a place more or less of her choice.

You are in your local bar with a mate and your girlfriend discovers that unknown to you, your previous girlfriend's car is parked outside your apartment. She sends you a text:

F: 'Her car is outside your house' [Female Adult or Child]

M: No response – no matter how many times this kind of text is sent. [Male Parent Withdrawal Deterrent]

F: 'Where are you?' [Female Adult or Parent]

You can respond in a number of ways to this, all of which put into effect a Withdrawal Deterrent:

M: No response

Or:

M: 'Why?'

Or:

M: '?'

Or:

M: 'I don't understand the question'

All of these are Parent responses with degrees of Withdrawal. Failing to get a satisfactory response, she then wants to come to the bar and see you in person:

F: 'I thought I would come over and join you both' [Parent]

Once again, a number of Male Parent responses are possible, all of which display a Withdrawal Deterrent:

M: No response

Or:

M: 'This is not for you love' [Parent Boundary Setting]

Or:

M: 'You are not invited' [Parent/Adult Boundary Setting]

Female catfights

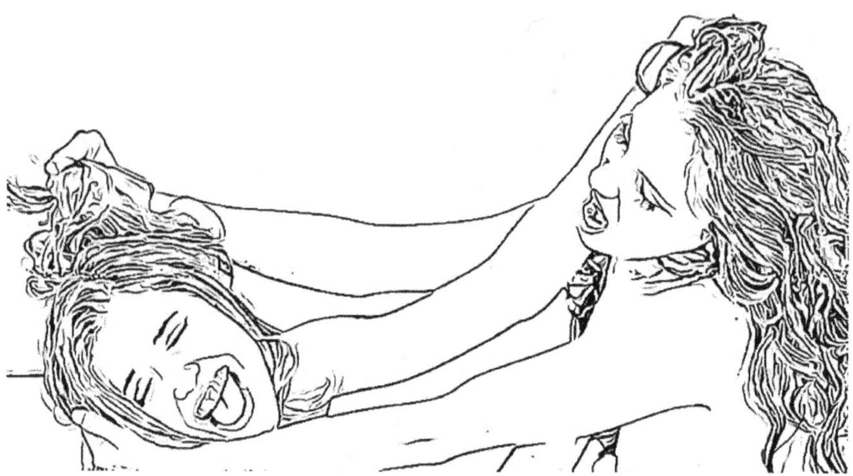

If your girlfriend wants to catfight – leave her to it. Don't be drawn into it. Ignore such squabbles - you don't have to find solutions or comprehend what is said - it is the 'white noise' of 'emotional intelligence'. Your girlfriend *will* try to draw you in to the Dark Continent of the emotional sphere, but if asked for your opinion you say that you **don't care** to give your opinion and **don't care** about the squabble [Parent].

You may decide to walk away [Withdrawal Deterrent]. If she challenges you then you say that you walk where and when you like [Parent] and walk away.

If she tries to get you to make a choice, say between her and the girl she is fighting with, you can indeed make a choice and support the female you like best, but you tell her that you don't want to listen to all this stuff about her jealousy any more. [Boundary Setting] If she insists on talking about your ex-girlfriends then tell her again that you are not prepared to listen and walk away [Withdrawal Deterrent].

Or, faced with a continued catfight, get a ringside seat and offer to sell tickets to spectators [Male Parent].

You may step in right at the very end of the fight when one female is obviously beaten, to rescue her from being killed, but that is about it [Male Parent].

If the conflict carries on at an annoyingly low level, with her trading insults, suspicions and bad-mouthing either you or your ex, [Child], you may decide that she is not making you happy and walk away anyway:

> M: 'I can only be honest, speak my heart and say what I feel. I can do no other.' [Communication at the emotional level – so she will understand that this is the bottom line – it is how you *feel*] 'I am who I am and I'm just unable and unwilling to change.' [Honesty – another good ploy] 'You're not capable of keeping me happy – you are not capable of keeping *me*. This relationship is finished. It's out of my control.' [Parent Withdrawal Deterrent].

Telling lies – always a mistake

You have jobs to do and tell your girlfriend that you won't be able to see her on Saturday. She's not happy but reluctantly agrees. But on the day it turns out that you manage to do the work sooner than you expected and at the end of the afternoon your mates give you an invitation to go out for a drink. Work is done and the invite is too  tempting to miss. That night, your girlfriend, thinking that you are still working, sends a text asking what you are doing. Knowing that she's unhappy at not seeing you, you also know that she will be very angry if she finds out that you are out drinking – so you tell a lie – and make out that you are still at home working.

Later she discovers the truth and is furious. She won't let you forget it – and starts calling you 'Pinocchio'. Every time you say you are doing something, she questions it:

> F: 'Are you really going out shopping today or are you out drinking with your mates Pinocchio?' [Critical Parent]

She **has no hesitation in** using your misbehavior against you. She does not think that you might be offended, get angry or even finish the relationship. She's straight in with the knife so that you don't forget your misdemeanors.

She can also use this tactic of using your misbehavior against you so that she can take your focus away from *her* misbehaviors.

Therefore, don't hesitate to use similar tactics on her:

> M: 'No, I am out shopping. What are you doing?' [Adult]

> F: 'I have gone to London for the day with my friend Susan'

> M: 'How do I know that you are not with someone else? Are you telling me the truth?'

> F: '*You* were the one caught lying'

> M: 'Perhaps *you* haven't been caught yet'. [Parent with humor]

Telling lies is always a mistake. With this particular situation you have to apologize - but also make it very clear where your personal boundary line is. You have what females call a 'heart to heart' talk - what males call a 'face to face' or 'head to head'. You admit that you told a lie and that you were wrong. You can partly justify this *by saying that you were thinking about her feelings*:

> M: 'I told you a lie because I knew you were unhappy about not seeing me on Saturday and I didn't want to upset you any more'. [Adult]

You see? You use the kind of emotional/feeling talk that she readily understands and express your concern about how she feels.

> M: 'But I am sorry – it was wrong of me to lie to you' [Adult]

This draws a line under the matter – if she keeps on going on about it she's in danger of showing unacceptable behavior herself.

If you tell lies you undermine her trust in you, and her trust in you is vital. But this kind of conversation also provides you with an opportunity to establish or re-establish your personal boundaries:

> M: 'But the fact is this – if I want to go out for a drink with my mates, then that's my choice. I don't need *your* permission either to go out or to change my mind and do something different.' [Parent Boundary Setting]

6 CREATING AND KEEPING PERSONAL BOUNDARIES

Define yourself – who you are, what you stand for, what your goals are, what your personal moral code is and so on. This way you also define who and what you are not – 'I love beef therefore I am not a vegetarian'. These self-definitions create your personal boundary lines. If anyone crosses these lines they steal your authority and self-determination – they are trying to change who you are. When someone tells you in a teacher-like tone of voice that you should be a vegetarian, or if they treat you with scorn because you eat meat, or if they keep choosing vegetarian meals for you - they step over the line.

Establish your boundaries and boundary rules

The power and control you have in a relationship depends on you keeping your boundaries and boundary rules in place. This book is not about how to dominate or manipulate your girlfriend, it is about you maintaining your self-control and self-determination – and this means that you don't allow her (or anyone else) to take power and control from you by stepping over these lines.

Your boundary rules set limits on how other people behave

in relation to you, and let people know where they stand. In particular, this involves teaching and training your girlfriend in terms of how you expect to be treated, by pointing out the boundaries between her acceptable and unacceptable behavior and attitudes. If she crosses these lines and rules there are deterrents that you will apply. Your boundary rules give structure to your relationships.

Talking to other females

With new girlfriends, it's important to establish very early on that you talk to other females even though she may be present. You don't expect fits of jealousy, or any arguments, sulks and so on later on [Female Child]. When you are seen talking with other females, this raises your attractiveness, and at the end of the day, you return home with your girlfriend – so indirectly, her esteem is raised too.

Rigid or flexible boundaries?

Your boundaries can be fixed or flexible – it's up to you. If you put a lot of rigid boundaries in place, chances are your relationship won't last long. What at first seems to be your masterful strength and principled decision-making will soon be seen as inflexible arrogance and selfishness. Make this choice up front. You can be totally committed to being the person you are and refuse to compromise – and thus probably have short-term relationships, or if the relationship continues, be dominant and overbearing to your downtrodden girlfriend. Or you can accept that long-term relationships need compromises - part of the price you pay - so you agree to modify some aspects of who you are and how you behave.

Making open and straightforward compromises [Adult] is not a problem. You both agree what is mutually acceptable or unacceptable and boundaries are agreed and roles and responsibilities are allocated to each person.

Unfortunately, girlfriends don't usually stick to the agreed rules - being emotionally led, sooner or later her 'Emotional Intelligence' will take over and she will complain that you are inflexible because you follow the rules (that you both agreed together). In Adult you may decide that you can be flexible and move your goalposts to accommodate her. Not a problem. But what may happen over time, unnoticed by you, is that you move your goalposts a foot here, then later a foot there, a couple of inches now, a few more inches in the future, **until your goal ends up being as wide as the entire width of the pitch** so that no matter what you do, she kicks the ball into the back of your net every time.

In this way, over time, you allow your boundary lines to be changed to a point where you have scored an own goal. You have been too flexible and not successfully maintained your boundaries, as you would like them to be. What begins as a flexible approach of small compromises ends up with your boundary control being usurped.

Boundary maintenance

Place a ring fence around your core values, principles and ideals so that you and you alone control and set the agenda in these areas. Constantly patrol and monitor your boundary and put alarms and sirens on it to alert you in your head when she tries to take charge of these areas. Refuse to allow any boundary transgressions. For example, never, ever, allow females to presume to give you unasked for advice. Maintaining this ring fence and repelling all intruders will keep you one up.

Lack of boundary setting

Girlfriends will insist that you 'do your share of tidying' in the house. But:

They do not define who does what, leaving the responsibility for many tasks vague

She will then blame you for her own failures. If she hasn't dusted the furniture, she blames you for failing to clean around the house, saying that you don't look, don't care, don't pull your weight or don't do a fair share of the work.

Some girlfriends may decide that *she* tidies away *her* things while you tidy away your things –

> F: 'They are *your* slippers – *you* should put them away!' [Parent setting your boundaries]

So you put your slippers by the side of the sofa - convenient for you to put on and off. Your girlfriend, using a hidden plan known only to her, then says:

> F: 'They do *not* go there!' [Parent setting your boundaries]

Or:

> F: 'That's what you call tidying up is it?' [Parent setting your boundaries]

In this situation, the cleaning rules have not been well defined. There are a number of ways out of this. In Adult, you can both clearly set out such rules, though as we have seen, she may want to randomly change these rules.

Or, in Parent, you can take charge of what *you* do:

> M: 'If *I* am tidying up, my slippers go *here*!' [Parent Boundary Setting]

If she insists on continually correcting you, then you can say:

> M: 'Since you obviously have high standards and I don't seem able to meet them, *you* can take responsibility for the cleaning! That way you will meet your own high standards.' [Parent Boundary Setting]

Any unacceptable responses from her will mean that you activate deterrents. But it's important to keep a balance. Being 'one up' is not about you always winning boundary rule arguments. You can afford to give her small victories, letting her win an occasional battle, because your eye is on the whole campaign rather than a mere skirmish.

Establish your boundary rules

Even with a short-term relationship, set up your boundary rules and as soon as necessary, communicate them to your girlfriend to establish what you think of as 'bad' or 'undesirable' behavior on her part. In a short-term relationship there are only two rules:

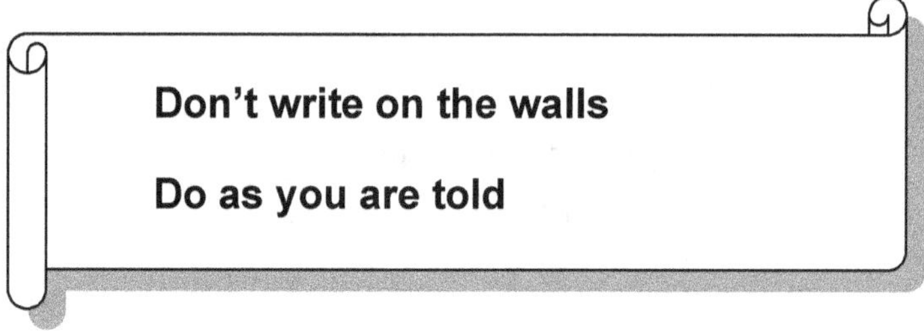

For long-term relationships, get together in Adult to define your mutually agreed boundary rules as the relationship gets serious. You always establish boundary rules when both of you are in Adult. They are a business contract defining limits within the relationship. In business, when discussing contracts, you don't become 'superior'; or become a clown. Your communication is direct, honest and straightforward. You don't play 'games'; you aren't underhanded.

When establishing shared boundary rules, you *don't* <u>have</u> to compromise

Having to compromise is not part of the deal.

If she breaks the rules later on, in Adult and in a direct, open way you get her to take responsibility for her actions or lack of them. You portray her breaking of the rules as a betrayal, a breaking of the contract that means you have every right to be angry.

If she breaks the rules but then refuses to move into Adult in order to discuss the matter, you move into Parent in response. You withdraw your humor and become the authoritarian, disciplinarian Parent to her 'naughty little girl' or her presumptuous 'superior' Parent.

Remember!

This works both ways!

This is the case if *you* break the rules too!

In Adult you are not 'one up' so be aware of the **'democratic equality' trap**. You are still in control of and in charge of yourself so it is *you* that draws the line when it comes to if and how far and how often *you* make compromises.

If your girlfriend puts pressure on you to go beyond this point, if she moves beyond reasoned discussion into attempts to control you, you need to be ready to say 'this far - and no farther.'

Many males constantly compromise their own preferences because they fear that if they oppose their girlfriend they will lose her. Such males operate from weakness. Remember - YOU are the prize that *she* will lose if she does not learn to behave and respect your preferences. You need to operate from strength. If you have been over-compromising or operating from a weak position - you can still change **if** you make up your mind to do so. It's never too late to take control of yourself again.

But in response to this, she will increase her attempts to control you and regain power. But if your mind is made up and you are wise to her tactics, you can start to bring things into balance again.

Your boundary rules cover anything from domestic duties, other relationships, personal preferences, personal hobbies and projects and so on. They cover who does what - who does the cooking, the washing up and the ironing for example. They cover the financial contributions of each partner, who is responsible for sorting out the bills and so on. You personally will establish some rules as being without question (and vice-versa). If you don't want to be phoned at work, then that is your rule. It is not acceptable for her to break the rule except for real emergencies, and it is not open to discussion. She may have some unquestionable rules too. If you can't accept her rules, don't get into the relationship or move any closer - itself a form of Withdrawal Deterrent.

Female training: Rewards and deterrents male style

You train your girlfriend to behave in a way and to a standard that you expect. Never tolerate 'bad', 'undesirable' or 'unacceptable' behavior or attitudes from her and always apply deterrents when such behaviors or attitudes occur.

It may seem small-minded to use deterrents every time, but she notches up every single bit of misbehavior that you do, but she will surprisingly forget all about her own misbehaviors. When it comes to having an argument, if she is in the wrong, she will recall lots of examples of your misbehavior to put you on the defensive. So don't have any hesitation about telling her when she is at fault.

Deterrents usually involve withdrawal – like not phoning or not sending texts as you usually do. If she texts to ask if she's done something wrong, a sharp 'No' is all you need reply - no smiley faces, no kisses - and you send this reply after some delay. When you next meet her, restate your boundary rule, giving her clear communication of the boundary *you had already established:*

> M: 'I thought that we had already gone over this - I do not want to be phoned at work'. [Critical Parent]

Arguments and fall-outs

Insisting on maintaining boundary rules may lead to arguments. If you have established boundary rules and you have followed them properly yourself - these arguments must be *her* fault.

You may be very tempted to let her small misbehaviors go without comment, to keep a quiet, easy life. But her constant drip, drip, drip of small crossing of boundary rules will eventually lead to the complete erosion of your boundaries. You may not keep score of small misdemeanors, but she is certainly keeping a score of *your* failings. So, be prepared for arguments.

Here are some simple tips and hints -

Facing her breaking of boundary rules honestly and head on may sound confrontational but this is not about hostility. But you do oppose her breaking established rules and if she *has* broken a rule then she is responsible. In trying to sort this issue out, don't confuse her *as a person* with what she has done: you are not critical of *her*, you are critical of her *behavior*.

If one or the other of you can't stay in Adult then the discussion may well deteriorate. If she won't move to Adult then you must move to Parent, and adopt an authoritarian, disciplinarian, superior, scolding attitude.

It can be helpful to carry out serious arguments by text messaging, because when she replies, you will have definite evidence of what she has said. Also, she can't interrupt or sidetrack the argument as easily, or drag you into the emotional swamp. Having to compose a text message means you have time to give a good, well thought out response and you can finish the argument at any time by simply not responding. The disadvantage is that you have no facial expressions or tones of voice to pick up on, so text messages can easily be misinterpreted.

If you have a sexual relationship, your girlfriend withdrawing sex as part of an argument isn't an option – it's 'unacceptable behavior'. If you aren't living together and she tries this tactic, leave, for that night at the very least. Put your coat on and go through the door. If she accuses you of always thinking about sex, you can reply:

M: 'That's because you are so desirable'. [Emotional

argument in order to connect with her passion]

This response appeals to her Child, **but you still leave anyway** unless she apologizes and changes her mind.

In arguments, girlfriends are often openly emotional because they are not in Adult. She will quickly move to emotions and try to drag you there as well. This would be to your disadvantage because males operate first and foremost in the 'thinking' realm and not the emotional realm. If she turns the argument into an emotional one and draws you into emotional rather than cognitive responses, she will have the advantage and you will be 'one down'.

She will also go down sidetracks when arguing. Your argument may be about being phoned at work but she will soon include arguments about how lazy you are, how rude you were to her mother and so on. Her 'emotional intelligence' leads her down these detours and her 'present moment' thinking means she will say the first emotional thing that spills over into her awareness.

The rule when it comes to arguments is:

Stay focused and keep her focused on the issue at hand

In the argument about phoning you at work she may say:

> F: 'And another thing! You never wash the dishes....'
> [Parent, Distraction, Tangent]

> M: 'I'm not interested in dishes – I'm interested in the
> fact that you phoned me at work when I told you not
> to.' [Focused Critical Parent]

Here is another rule:

Never reward her with treats or presents

after an argument as part of 'making up'

It looks like you are rewarding her unacceptable behavior or even rewarding the fact that she has argued with you at all. Any treats and rewards that you give to her must be delayed by at least a couple of days after making up, to prevent any link in her mind between arguments, making up and rewards.

If you are full of anger [Child] with her, reign in and control your Child response by using your Adult and Parent. If you 'throw a wobbly' and throw things about or shout it can either be very funny or very frightening to her. Neither reaction is good. If she finds your anger funny or even pathetic it's because you've suddenly become a Child having a temper tantrum - as frightening and authoritative as a four year old. When you begin to calm down she may say:

> F: 'Feeling better now?' [Sarcastic Nurturing Parent]

And so you explode into another fit of temper. She may merely laugh at these tantrums. You've moved almost completely to Child and entered the emotional realm that she knows far better than you. Your rational Adult and 'superior' Parent have gone out of the window and you may be irrational, unpredictable, spiteful and bullying. If you are physically tall and or strong, this may be very scary for her and you may be in danger of lashing out. Walk away and express your anger on an object (not the family pet) to diffuse it.

If you can express your anger by using your Parent/Adult this is much better, as we shall see below. Instead of being over-emotional, you are detached from the emotional realm she wants to drag you into and so you don't raise your voice, don't show rage, and don't even tell her off. Instead, you speak with a deadly quietness that gives an impression of barely contained violent wrath. Males in Adult or Parent don't quarrel. Instead you state your opinion of her, her actions, her house and her friends – so she has no doubt, because what you say has only one meaning.

Arguments - Volume and pitch of the female voice

When she emotionally defends what she has done or said, her voice may rise in pitch – almost to squealing as well as rising in volume.

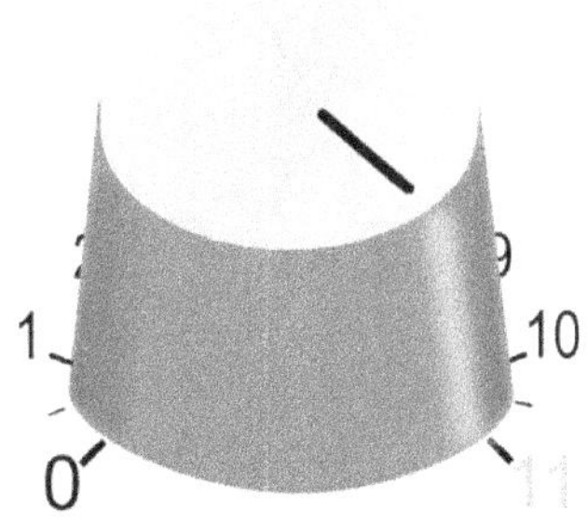

Her high-pitched and/or loud voice is her attempt at dominance. If you become aware of either of these you can calmly point them out:

> M: 'Calm it down love – you're squealing'. [Parent with humor]

Or:

> M: 'Steady sweetheart – you're becoming hysterical'. [Parent with humor]

Or:

> M: 'Are you all right? You seem a bit agitated'. [Parent with humor]

Better still, use gestures and don't say a word, like putting a raised finger to your mouth to indicate that she should speak in quieter tones.

In an argument, always remember:

> **You are the prize**
>
> **Avoid feelings of guilt - stay detached**
>
> **Stay focused**
>
> **Keep her focused on the issue**
>
> **Don't reward her unacceptable behavior**
>
> **Always use deterrents**
>
> **Speak with barely contained anger**
>
> **Can't control your anger? Walk away**

Some examples of boundary crossing and boundary maintenance

She must never call at your house or apartment uninvited or unexpectedly. Never reward this behavior by answering the door - you may even escape through the back door and get to your local bar, so that when she phones you can apologize, say you are at the bar and she can meet you there. The rule is:

She only calls at your house or apartment when it is convenient for you and arranged by you

In this way you retain control.

Here's another example – She hides your keys as a bit of fun [Child]. When you have recovered your keys tell her plainly that *you don't like misplacing your keys and you don't expect her to do that again* [Parent]. If she *does* do it again, remind her of the rule and leave for the rest of the day - or even finish the relationship.

Another example – You've had a meal at home together and she offers to wash the dishes. You don't want her to because you have some delicate wine glasses in the sink that you don't want to be broken.

> F: 'I'll wash the dishes.' [Adult]

> M: 'No it's O.K. - I'll wash the dishes later.' [Adult]

> F: 'No, you have prepared the meal, so I'll do the dishes.' [Adult/Child]

> M: 'No! I don't want you to do the dishes – I'll do them.' [Emphatic Parent/Adult]

You go to get some wine from another room and while you are out she starts to wash the dishes [Defiant Child]. She's trying to do you a favor in return for cooking the meal but she has either not heard what you've said or feels the need to wash the dishes despite what you've said - she feels she can get around you [Child]. In this case, put your hands on her shoulders, guide her away from the sink to a chair and give her towel to dry her hands. [Male Parent]

> M: 'Look, you're pissing me off now!' [Coupled with broad charming smile to avoid conflict]. 'I don't want to fall out with you - sit down there and make yourself

comfortable with a glass of wine.' [Critical Male Parent]

Sometimes this kind of situation may be your fault for not laying down the rules firmly enough and this is why she has not heard you or feels that she can get around you.

Mission Creep – opportunistic tactics

Girlfriends spy opportunities to cross your boundaries, and use emotional tactics to get their own way. For example, Adam recently met Annabelle, who soon became his 'girlfriend'. Adam decided to move out of the apartment he rented with a male friend, to get his own property. Very quickly, Annabelle suggested that she could move in with him – help him with the rent etc, etc.

Your girlfriend will not like you having your own apartment or house etc. Why? Because she has *no control* over what happens there and you have a place that you can withdraw to. The walls and doors are a clear statement of your personal boundary line. What happens inside is your business, not hers, and she has no say about it. Once that door is shut you are king of your own domain. If she misbehaves, you can execute the Withdrawal Deterrent of returning to the sanity of your own property – or throw her out of it.

A friend pointed out to Adam that: 'She will be in your apartment by the autumn and you will be engaged by Christmas!' It seems so innocent – let her to move in and help with the rent – it flatters your male pride and if you refuse, she will get emotional in the arena of the dreaded 'C' word – Commitment:

> F: 'Aren't you serious about us?'

> F: 'Doesn't our relationship mean anything to you?'

> F: 'I thought [read 'felt'] that we were building a relationship together'

> F: 'Of course, if you don't want to be with me....'

Before you know it there'll be scented candles in your rooms and so many scatter cushions on your bed it will take you ten minutes to get into it. In winter, windows will be flung open to 'let some air in' as the cozy warmth evaporates and temperatures descend to near-freezing as a gale blows through the room.

Remember this – your home or apartment is your castle, a well-fortified defense. Remote controls stay where you left them and your favorite chair is not moved, sat in or altered in any way. Invite her in to stay with you for a few days and – as you open the door, like a flash, she will step in and stand behind you with a knife at your back. All your defensive walls, your carefully maintained and patrolled personal boundary lines, and the watchtowers that you set up to monitor and sound the alarm when border crossings occurred – and what have you done? You have opened up the front door wide allowing her to step in behind the fence.

If she has crossed a Boundary, your *only* option is to re-establish your Boundary Line so she is in no doubt as to where the perimeter fence lies. If you sense that things are going too fast, that she is setting the pace without consulting you, that you are being cornered – alarm bells need to ring loudly in your head and you need to check the perimeter fence. If she has crossed the line you need to deal with it. Better still – nip it in the bud.

A close female friend arrives unexpectedly, and upset:

> F: 'I had an argument with my boyfriend and I had to sleep in my car overnight.' [Vulnerable Child]

> M: 'That must have been uncomfortable'. [Male Parent/Adult]

> F: 'I can't face him again. Can I stay at your house tonight?' [Vulnerable Child]

> M: 'No. It is too soon. I don't feel ready for such a commitment yet' [Male Adult]

> F: 'Don't you love me?' [Vulnerable Child]

> M: 'I love you very much, but I don't feel ready to commit like this yet. That's how I feel. I'm only human – I'm telling you where I am at the moment. If you don't like it then its up to you what you choose to do.' [Male Parent]

> F: 'I'm scared to face him after the argument we had.' [Vulnerable Child]

> M: 'Do you want me to talk to him and tell him how things are?' [Male Parent]

F: 'No! No!' [Vulnerable Child]

M: 'Shall I help you to find a hotel room for the night?' [Adult]

Or:

M: 'Shall I find a hotel room for you for tonight?' [Parent]

You have to deal with this kind of sneaky crossing of boundaries immediately and it requires constant alertness on your part. You can't let your guard down for one second with these kinds of attempts. Being aware of her tactics is the first step. You may seem cruel but you are being *honest* and this could save you from greater heartache in the future. If you can express your thoughts and evaluations not only honestly, but as *feelings* – 'I don't *feel* ready to commit' instead of 'I don't *think* I'm ready to commit' - you will communicate your boundaries very well, because you will be talking her language.

Crossing boundaries – Unasked for advice

There is worse to come. Girlfriends not only:

Give unasked for advice

Make decisions for you and

Cross your boundaries

But in addition:

Girlfriends don't take responsibility for the advice they give and decisions they take

If you follow her advice and end up with problems it won't be her fault.

No way

Guess what pal – it will be *your* fault. *You* carry the can sonny.

Girlfriends are unable to take responsibility for their decisions and advice. If you follow her advice to the letter and then it goes pear-shaped, she will find something, *anything*, that you did or said that will let her 'off the hook'.

Crossing boundaries – Assertive female Parent

Some girlfriends in Parent become very assertive in their opinions and in their demands that you explain yourself.

> F: 'What is this baby doing with an apple?' [Parent in teacher-like tone of voice]

She indirectly imposes her agenda – 'I don't feel that this baby should have an apple' [Boundary crossing]. She is pressurizing the person who gave the baby an apple to explain why – [Justification trap].

You can deal with this by openly taking responsibility for your decision in equally assertive and emotional terms:

> M: 'I *felt* the baby would *enjoy* an apple' [Parent]

This is as much self-explanation as you ever need to give. How you feel is the bottom line as far as she is concerned. But she may well challenge you again by restating her felt agenda in parental tones:

> F: 'Babies shouldn't have apples' [Parent]

Or:

> F: 'What a silly thing to do – giving baby an apple!' [Critical Parent in disdainful tones]

Then you **really** re-assert your boundary lines:

> M: 'He/she is *my* baby. I don't have to explain to *you* what I choose to do' [Parent Boundary Setting]

Or:

> M: 'He/she is my baby. **I don't care** what you think/feel, I don't have to explain to you what I choose to do' [Parent Boundary Setting]

Some examples of deterrents

We have seen that withdrawing yourself can be an effective deterrent.

For example, your girlfriend is sulking [Female Child] because you have been tickling her [Male Child]. (This is your mistake because you have moved to Child). Even so, you respond to her sulk within four or five minutes and say you are going home. Put your coat on and leave. [Male Parent Withdrawal Deterrent]

If her behavior is seriously bad, extend this deterrent and remain absent for the night with no explanations or apologies [Parent]. When you *do* return, if she responds by arguing or sulking again [Child], withdraw until suppertime [Parent]. If she still sulks, [Child] go away for a few days and return with a cool attitude [Parent]. Ultimately, if she can't behave herself then you withdraw completely.

Here's another example - You cancel a date with your girlfriend because you are tired and need some space on your own. Later, you go to your local bar for a drink and a live band is playing. You text your girlfriend to tell her how enjoyable the music is and that you are finally unwinding. She texts back:

> F: 'It's alright for you to enjoy yourself while I sit here by myself.' [Child]

> M: 'Sorry, Look, I was only sharing my enjoyment. I won't bother in the future'. [Parent]

Here, 'sorry' doesn't mean sorry. When people say 'Yes but' they are dismissing all that has been said before. In the same way 'Sorry, Look...' means I am not sorry and I am laying down the rules. [Parent]. Your response is immediate and the deterrent is withdrawal. You don't buy a dog and expect it to bite you. You are in this relationship for your pleasure and if there is no pleasure (and no sex), what is all the rest for?

You can withdraw your interest in her and what she has done or said -

> F: 'I had a great time last night' [Child]

> M: 'Really' [Spoken with a disdainful tone] [Parent]

Or:

> F: 'How do I look in this?' as she tries a dress on that

you don't like.

M: 'O.K.' Spoken with matter of fact tones and disinterest. [Parent]

Or:

M: 'Nice' [Faint praise]

Disapproval is another effective deterrent, especially if you can learn to just raise an eyebrow, give a disapproving look, a curl of the mouth or disapproving tone of voice.

Some examples of rewards

Rewards include arriving with chocolates and champagne, putting her photo as the background image on your phone - (it can just as easily be removed), cooking a romantic meal, buying her clothes, surprise holidays, buying flowers and so on. It is good practice to cook her a romantic meal once or twice a year. It is all about making her the center of attention and indulging her Child vanity.

The 'I was only joking' ploy

When you catch your girlfriend attempting to get one up on you, or you strongly challenge her, she may retreat to the **'I was only joking' ploy** and try to dismiss what she's said or done. You may not find what she's done or said to be very funny – so don't laugh along with her 'joke' [Withdrawal Deterrent]. The last thing to do is to reassure her that everything is all right – it isn't. So you don't say things like:

'That's O.K., forget it!'

Or:

> 'Don't worry about it – I love you to bits.'

You stay in Parent and continue to withdraw your humor, and present instead an attitude of detachment. A good strategy is to respond to her in a vague, detached and disapproving way by simply saying 'Hmmm' or 'I see' in a disdainful way. She needs to see that you are 'marking her card' so that in her mind she sees you 'making a note in her personal file' like a headmaster – for future reference. But your words are vague *so that she can project her anxieties and fears onto the uncertainties of what you say*.

Cultivating a 'good girl'

It's amusing to use the phrase 'good girl' when she does something you approve of. For example, after a meal she gathers the dishes and takes them into the kitchen -

> F: 'I'll take the dishes.'

> M: 'Thanks very much. Good girl!' [Parent]

The phrase is best delivered with a smile [Male Parent using Child humor]. She may openly challenge you, but you challenge her in return and say: 'But you **are** a good girl.' Make sure to use this phrase at least once on every date. When this was done in practice, after a few weeks, a girlfriend started to sarcastically *call herself* a good girl -

F: 'I'll take the dishes - I'm a good girl.'

M: 'Yes you are!' (Smiles). [Combination of Parent with Child humor]

The 'good girl' strategy has three phases:

Call her a 'good girl' at least once on every date

She starts to call *herself* a 'good girl'

She asks **you** whether she is a 'good girl' without prompting from you -

F: 'Am I a good girl?' [Child]

M: 'Yes you are!' [Parent]

Ever changing boundaries and situations

You change, situations change and so do boundary rules. You may not be aware of the need to change your boundary lines until something happens that brings it into focus. Here are a couple of examples:

It turns out that you now have the chance to finish work an hour earlier every week on Fridays, so you decide to go to your bar to enjoy a quiet drink. You decide not to tell your girlfriend [Adult] - you know she won't approve and begin to nag you [Critical Parent]. But she finds out and starts to argue with you. She says it's not the going to the bar that's the problem, **it's that you lied about it and deceived her.**

Your girlfriend might even say that it's not the fact that you went with another female, but that you deceived her. This is a **detour** or blatant lie. If you decided to respond by saying, 'O.K., I'll be honest: from now on, I'll be going to bed with another female every Wednesday', there are few girlfriends who will say 'That's O.K., at least you are honest'.

So ignore her deceitful 'if only you had told me about it' tactic. She does not want you to go to the bar. You have to re-establish the boundary rules.

> M: 'If I choose to go to the bar for an hour on Friday after work, I will. I'm back home at the same time, it doesn't concern you.' [Parent/Adult]

She may offer a number of responses but the bottom line for you is....

> M: 'If you aren't happy with this, you can leave.' [Threat of Withdrawal Deterrent]

Try to learn **never saying 'sorry'**. Many males have been brought up to think that it's good manners to apologize, **even if they're not wrong**. They apologize for other people's emotions - 'Sorry you're crying'. Make the effort to avoid this word. Saying 'sorry' can be so deeply learned that we do it without thinking, so become aware of how often you use it. Then you can start to replace it with alternatives.

So **don't** say:

> 'Sorry I'm late'.

Rather say:

> M: 'I got held up at work' [Adult. Vague justification - give as few reasons as possible] 'I hope I didn't

inconvenience you.' [Adult. Empathic concern]

Or **don't** say:

'I'm sorry you are crying'

Rather say:

M: 'I don't want to see you upset.' [Adult]

Remember:

You are not responsible for her emotions

She is responsible for how she feels.

Some examples of weak male responses

Doubts? Consider this factual case of a male operating in a weak way.

About 8.00 to 8.30 in the morning, phone calls inconveniently arrive while the male is at work. He feels that he must reply immediately.

F: 'Am I seeing you tonight?'

Weak M: 'No, sorry. I'm seeing my friends'.

F: 'So! You'd rather see your mates than me?'

Weak M: 'Sorry, but it's been arranged for a while.'

F: 'Oh....right....' Puts the phone down.

He feels he has to ring her back to smooth things over and gain her approval again.

Here is another example:

On the day of a first, loosely arranged evening date, texts inconveniently arrive while he is at work. He feels he must reply immediately.

> F: 'What time are we meeting?'

> Weak M: '8.00?'

> F: 'Can we make it 7.30?'

> Weak M: 'O.K.'

She asked a question, was given an answer, but wants to change it, (possibly revealing that she is in Parent). In Adult, she might have said: 'What time are we meeting? I would prefer 7.30. How about you?' But here, she is trying to set the agenda for him [Parent]. She disagrees with **whatever** he says, usurping his stated preferences and role, whilst seeking to dictate the agenda. Notice also how quickly she uses this approach - **even before the first date**.

Alternative strong male responses

Here are the same situations dealt with using a strong male Parent approach coupled with principles I've outlined earlier:

About 8.00 to 8.30, phone calls inconveniently start to arrive while he is at work. The [strong] male does not feel that he must reply immediately.

F: 'Am I seeing you tonight?' [Adult or Parent]

After some considerable delay, [Parent, Withdrawal Deterrent] he gives his reply:

Strong M: 'No'. [Parent - No explanation]

Or alternatively, if he is in Adult position and gives reasons for his answer:

M: 'No. I'm seeing my friends'. [Adult]

F: 'So! You'd rather see your mates than me?' [Parent]

She uses the **justification trap** as her point of attack. He replies:

Strong M: 'Tonight yes, I would rather see my friends.' [Parent]

F: 'Oh....right....' Puts the phone down. [Child - snubbed vanity]

He then decides that she will **definitely** not see him tonight because she has behaved unacceptably by putting the phone down on him [Male Parent, Withdrawal Deterrent]. He may even terminate the relationship. [Male Parent, Withdrawal Deterrent] If he *does* see her again, he will explain his boundary rules to her once more, face to face. [Male Parent/Adult], and say that if she hangs up on him again, the relationship will be over [Withdrawal Deterrent, Boundary Setting].

Or, alternatively, when the first inconvenient text arrives, the strong male may text:

Strong M. 'I'm at work, I will talk later' [Parent, Withdrawal Deterrent]

Or:

Strong M: 'I'm trying to work here.' [Indignant Parent dismissal]

On seeing her later, he would establish boundary rules about being sent texts or phoned at work [Male Parent/Adult]. He may state that if it happens again, the relationship will be over [Withdrawal Deterrent].

In the second of the two weak male scenarios, on the day of the first, loosely arranged date, inconvenient texts start to arrive while he is at work.

F: 'What time are we meeting?'

The [strong] male does not feel that he must reply immediately. After some considerable delay the strong male replies:

Strong M: '8.00'

F: 'Can we make it 7.30?'

> Strong M: 'No' [Parent - no justification or explanation]

She has asked for a time, he has given it and now she wants to take over by trying to change it.

Or:

> Strong M: 'Make it 7.00 or not at all.' [Indignant Parent with threat of Withdrawal Deterrent].

Here he re-establishes his control of the agenda by setting a new time of his own choice for meeting up and declares that this is now the **only** option. On meeting her, he would establish boundary rules about being sent texts or being phoned at work [Male Parent/Adult].

In looking at the importance of setting and maintaining your boundary lines, we have begun to see some examples of countering her tactics so that you can stay one up.

Remember – If you are not one up, you are one down.

This leads us on to the next chapter, where we can look at examples of some responses that you can use in dealing with the various tactics that she will use to try and get one up and take away your control of your own life and agenda.

7 STAYING ON TOP - TACTICS

Counter strategies

We have seen that males and females are different in many ways, and that people act like a Parent, Adult or Child when they interact with other people. We have seen how these different positions reveal themselves in our speech and behavior. I suggested that in almost every case you are best acting like a Parent, to stop your girlfriend from taking over your life. Finally we looked at personal boundaries and your need to defend your boundaries against your girlfriend crossing the boundary line without permission. I suggested the use of Withdrawal Deterrents when she crossed your boundary line without permission. So, now it's time to look at some tactics and strategies in more detail so that you can stay one up.

Your quiz results should give you some idea of how you see your girlfriend - whether she tends to be in Parent, Adult or Child. Learn to recognize these three positions from moment to moment, by paying attention to what she says and how she says it - her tone of voice, posture, mannerisms and so on.

Dealing with 'emotional intelligence' and female logic

Your girlfriend tends to be more emotionally motivated - her Child position being the most emotional of all. If your girlfriend is mainly in Child you will have to deal with 'emotional intelligence'. So let's look at some strategies.

Females, intelligence and education

Females have an 'emotional mind' resulting in a particular form of reasoning called 'female logic'. Males tend to be the 'head' of the relationship and females tend to be the 'heart'.

Allowing your girlfriend to think, analyse, plan or make decisions to any great degree may well invite disaster and if she drags you into her realm of present-moment emotions you enter a swamp of confusion and darkness.

You may sometimes dismiss your girlfriend as being an empty-headed bimbo, not capable or intelligent. Big mistake. Some females are very intelligent, proving to be outstanding at science or mathematics - and intelligent females can be very attractive and sexy. There are females working in astrophysics; on projects associated with the Hadron Collider; in medicine, chemistry or any number of such fields. They may be the exception rather than the rule - and though logical and analytical at work, they may give in to their 'emotional intelligence' in other areas of their lives - especially when it comes to relationships.

So, as far as you are concerned, she doesn't take the lead in decision-making in your relationship. At the very least, she needs the balance that is supplied by your rational and thoughtful approach.

Decision making

Never – *ever* – let her make decisions

Your girlfriend may try to make decisions by taking over or leading conversations. On your very first date she may be filled with emotions about what a bastard her previous boyfriend was because he:

Didn't give her enough attention

Ate his food with his mouth open

Slurped his drinks

Failed to put the toilet seat down…..

……and so on.

She is already setting the agenda by indirectly telling you how she expects you to behave. If this happens and you are in a restaurant, open your wallet, put some money on the table and leave. If you are on the 'phone to her – hang up.

If she chases after you, tell her that you are not her previous boyfriend and refuse to sit back down at the table or keep talking. You are not a sponge to soak up her past failures. Tell her that you will get back to her, but right now you have to wash away the bad taste of how you have just been treated.

Here's another example: Imagine coming home from work to relax and watch the television and almost immediately your girlfriend tells you that she's arranged to go out to do some shopping. (She has also gained control of the household budget and bank account – you just contribute your hard earned cash). You ask if she's taking the children with her, and she says she isn't because you're at home so you can look after them. She's been waiting for you to come home so she can leave the kids with *you*.

Sometimes, in these situations, she says that she's told you she planned to go out - you must have forgotten. At other times, when *you've* planned to go out, surprise, surprise! – there's a clash of arrangements – she seems to have forgotten that she has arranged to go out as well - so you'll have to take the kids with *you*.

Here's a solution: Get a day-to-day wall chart planner and put it up in the kitchen. Tell her that this is to help her because you love her. This chart will help both of you to make clear arrangements written down on the wall planner.

You can play this a number of ways. You can countersign her arrangements so that she knows that you have seen what's happening and are happy with it. Countersigning anything that she writes will stop her ploy of putting her arrangements on the planner at short notice and making out that you didn't see it. If you don't countersign, it doesn't exist – it's a non-event, void.

Another approach is to use colored stickers – pink for her, blue for you. If the planner gets covered with pink you can question what's happening and insist on having some arrangements for yourself.

A wall chart suits your masculine outlook – set a goal and work towards it. Remember, girlfriends act in the 'here and now'. If they don't have a clear goal, they take action and set off in any random direction because they *feel* that they have to do *something*.

Decisions and opinions

Never ask your girlfriend questions that allow her to make major decisions, and never allow her to give you unasked for advice. Decisions about what **you** do or do not do are ***your*** domain. You can ask questions that allow her to form an *opinion*, but there's no way you ask her to voice any opinions about *you* – she'll do that soon enough all on her little own some. Instead, you her ask her opinions concerning safe, bland and mainly female themes like:

How to cook roast beef

Does this shirt match these trousers?

What was last year's best romantic movie?

How often should I water this plant?

When you ask her opinion on things like this it will feed the 'I need praise junkie' inside her. You give her the *illusion* of respecting her opinion.

But when it comes to unasked for advice – you might simply nod pleasantly - but do what you want anyway. If you constantly follow what she has to say like a three year old, this will breed her contempt of you.

When she makes questions and statements, she presents an *appearance* of logic and you may easily be fooled into thinking that she's seeking analysis, logic, concluding opinions, evaluation or a decision. Because cognition is your natural sphere, you will tend to be quick to step in with your analysis and solutions – which she does not want.

She's not being deliberately dishonest or sneaky – she's operating in her natural emotional sphere and unconsciously using 'emotional intelligence' resulting in 'female logic'. She uses 'logical' sounding words that seem to imply thought and conceptual analysis - but they are actually **emotional** statements.

When it comes to your own preferences you have an opinion and you can say it -

> F: 'Which do you prefer for roast dinner on Sunday - beef or lamb?'

> M: 'Beef - I *love* the taste of roast beef and beef gravy.'

State your preferences and opinions in **emotional** rather than cognitive terms. If she then asks -

> F: '**Why** do you prefer beef?' or '**What's wrong with** lamb?'

Don't give logical reasons - instead present your answer once again as an emotional preference -

M: 'Beef **satisfies** my taste buds like nothing else.'

She can't argue with your *emotional* response or personal *emotional* preference. She may have a different emotional preference and is entitled to it - but it doesn't undermine or take away your personal emotional preference for beef.

> # Respond to her questions by using
>
> # emotional terms and phrases

Decisions and responsibility

Girlfriends often want freedom to take charge – not only of their own life – but also of *you*. But:

> # Girlfriends deny responsibility and accountability for their decisions

They want to have authority and control until things go wrong and the results of their decisions, choices and leadership don't work out as they intended. Then they abandon responsibility and say things like:

F: 'That's your fault! Look what you made me do!' [Child]

When her decisions go wrong, she will often dump the consequences onto you.

Decisions, leadership and responsibility

If your girlfriend wants to take charge she *has* to take responsibility for her choices and actions. Learn to become skilled in the art of defining ownership. At work I found that the people who wanted to be bosses wanted better wages, more status, more privileges and sometimes more power and 'superiority' over other people. But when things in their department went wrong, they often *automatically* put the blame on the workers; or if there was a problem that they didn't want to face, they got one of the workforce to deal with it for them – 'Tell Bill to stop talking will you?' or if an area needed organizing, they tried to get the workers to sort it out for them.

It is the same with your girlfriend - she wants to be the leader but doesn't want to take responsibility. At work I learned the phrase: 'The manager's right to manage', so when a problem arose, I quickly decided whose problem it was – is it my problem because I have made a mistake, or is it a management problem, outside of my area of work? If it was the manager's problem I gave the manager the right to manage – they wanted to be a manager – so they can manage the problem – that's what they are paid extra wages for. In other words I quickly defined problem ownership and **set the boundaries** in my own mind. Is a member of staff talking too much? Don't ask me to have a word with them. Are absentee levels too high? Don't talk to those of us who are not absent – talk to those who keep failing to turn up. Is the department disorganized because of some planned rebuilding work? Not my problem – my problem is to carry on doing my job as efficiently as I can, not to organize the department.

Take the same approach with your girlfriend – quickly define whose problem it is. If she is organizing a particular area, such as getting the passports ready for a holiday, she *must* take responsibility for it.

> M: 'Did you pick up the passports?' [Adult]

> F: 'No! Do I have to think of *everything*?' [Child]

> M: 'No. You just had to remember the passports like we agreed.' [Parent/Adult]

By defining whose problem it is you avoid being dragged into problems that are not your concern - but it can be confrontational. At the very least it means facing her and pointing out ownership of the problem. If it is her problem it does not mean a lack of give and take. But it does mean that you don't allow your girlfriend to dump her failures on you.

If you think this is harsh, watch what happens when another female, such as your mother, steps in to tidy up your girlfriend's kitchen or home without asking her first. Believe me, your girlfriend will be quick to set her boundaries – this is *her* home and kitchen so *she* keeps it tidy! She will not allow any suggestion that her kitchen is untidy or dirty. There will either be an argument, a sulk, or both.

So what's good for the goose is good for the gander. You set and keep your boundary lines – make your own decisions, act on them, and take responsibility for them. **And so must she.**

Decisions and the illusion of leadership

Get your girlfriend used to the idea of you being the leader and decision-maker by starting with the small things.

Picture this - you both go to a café and you see that she is about to choose a table to sit at without asking you. **As soon as you see this** you suggest to her that this is the table you should sit at. You say: 'Let's sit at this table' and point to the table that she was about to choose. You have to do this a split second before she puts her choice into action – timing is all-important – if you are too late the strategy will fail. You anticipate what she is going to do, read the subtle cues that indicate her preference, and then suggest her own preference to her, in a cool, confident, relaxed leadership kind of way, before she has a chance to say it herself.

Decisions and female logic

'Women are like frogs – you never know which way they are going to jump'

Females operate primarily at an emotional level when it comes to relationships, 'girly-groups' and their status within these groups. This stuff is very important to them – how they present themselves in front of others and where they are in the pecking order in the group and so on.

They understand and negotiate their way through the world by using their emotions – how they 'feel' about the world around them, with a focus mainly on people and relationships rather than on 'things'. In the light of their feelings they make their choices. In the beginning, Eve *saw* (not thought) that the fruit was good and she *desired* it, *then* she thought about how to get it and eat it.

F: 'We don't laugh enough. That's our trouble. It's your fault. I think you were born angry. I don't like angry people.' [Child]

M: 'Seems like you don't think too much of me' [Parent Detachment]

F: '*I love you, so I don't care what I think of you.*' [Child Emotional Response]

Her feelings take primary place and then her thoughts and choices follow on as a result of how she feels. Her logical processes, *once the foundation of her emotions has been accepted*, are often structured and consistent – but her emotions may change at any time, and so her thinking and her decisions will change along with her emotions.

All of this is a largely alien domain to you. Most of her 'emotional intelligence' processes take place under the surface and are hidden from view, and in any case, you are not an emotional being but a *thinking* being. This by itself is enough to make you end up being bewildered by the choices she makes.

To make things even worse,

She describes her feelings

using cognitive terms

She will say 'I *think* it's terrible' instead of 'I *feel* terrible'.

How the hell can you get to the core of what she is feeling and why at any given moment?

Contrary to what she feels, you are not a mind reader. (She calls it **intuition**). You can see her emotions or pick up on her mood – she is crying, angry or whatever –

but this ain't enough information for you.

You don't know the hidden, underlying *reasons* for her emotional display - but she expects you to know - she expects you to use your 'intuition' and gets angry, frustrated and upset when you don't know. For you, this remains the unexplored Dark Continent.

Just when you think it couldn't get any worse, it does. Along come hormones. Females, to a greater degree than males, have monthly biological cycles – tidal waves of hormones rising and falling – and guess what – these strongly affect how she feels. These tidal waves assault the foundation of the way she sees and evaluates the world around her and in turn this affects her moods and her decision-making. But for her, all this moodiness and faulty thinking isn't ever her fault, therefore, guess what Clyde – it must be *your* fault. She may become irritable, accusing, over sensitive and generally appear to approach situations from the 'left field' – from a lateral direction that makes your brain almost seize up with a perplexed 'What?!?....Where the?!....How did we get?!?....What are you talking about?!?....'.

The last thing you do is become involved in any sort of argument – or 'discussion' as your girlfriend may prefer to call them. When faced with such an irrational, mood-dominated situation, the best thing you can do is put a Withdrawal Deterrent in place and leave. Her behavior and attitude, whether she knows it or not, is unacceptable. This is not the way you expect to be treated.

If you let her draw you into her 'discussion', you will be dragged lost and confused into the Dark Continent. (See map on previous page). Whatever negative emotions she experiences at this time will be your fault - she can't take ownership of these emotions, so it must be something to do with you.

So you put in place a Withdrawal Deterrent and leave. You don't storm out or argue with her. Instead, you quietly get up, take your coat and leave. You may say:

> 'I don't need this'

> 'I'll give you some time to yourself'

> 'I'll leave you to calm down'

Now she'll have something real to focus her irrational anger on – the fact that you left. And you *did* leave. It's an action you take responsibility for. You deal with any future accusations she makes by making out that you were doing her a favor – giving her the 'psychological and emotional space' she seemed to need – or whatever. If she carries on making more accusations, you leave again. [Withdrawal Deterrent]

Decisions and female 'logic' - Specific and particular or general and universal?

Be aware that your girlfriend may wildly alternate between **particular** events and **general** rules. If you stay out later than expected with your mates one night, she may say:

> 'You are *always* the same – you *never* think about me' [Child, All or nothing thinking]

Or:

> 'You men are *all* the same! You *always* put your mates before me!' [Child, All or nothing thinking]

Or:

> 'You *never* come home when you say you will!' [Child, All or nothing thinking]

She uses **general** rules and 'all or nothing thinking in her argument - words such as 'always', 'never' and 'all'. But if the situation is reversed and *she* stays out later than expected on a girly night out, when *you* are angry with *her*, she will move her argument to **particular** events:

> 'It was just a *one-off incident.*'

Or:

> 'I've only done it this *once*'

Or:

> 'It was Susan's twenty-first birthday' She is only

twenty one *once*!'

If your girlfriend sees you talking to a female friend of yours, she may **generalize** and say:

> F: 'You *never* talk to me like that! All smiles and dewy-eyed! You are *always* looking at pretty girls!'

But if you see her talking and laughing with a male who is a stranger to you, she will plead the **particular**:

> F: 'This is different! He is *only* an old school friend! We *only* had lunch and a drink at the restaurant because this is the first time I have seen him for twenty years'.

When this happens, you need to point it out to her so that she knows that you're not duped by her tactics.

Leadership versus stewardship

If both you and your girlfriend are trying to lead the relationship there will be conflict as you pull against each other - there can't be two leaders. Companies may have Boards of Directors but there is only one CEO.

Some feminists don't want males to be the 'head' of any aspect of the relationship – they want what looks at first sight to be a democracy - a relationship run by a committee of two. This reminds me of a saying:

'A camel is horse designed by a committee'

In other words, committees don't work very well. Worse still, feminists actually undermine this *appearance* of democracy and want to take charge and be the 'head' of the relationship themselves....until things go wrong, then, it will be *your* fault for not taking charge, or for distracting them!

Feminists *fear* that in allowing you to be the leader of the relationship, she will end up being dominated, isolated and enslaved. But it doesn't necessarily follow.

So what's the solution? Move away from the idea of leadership to the idea of 'responsible stewardship'. Since males and females operate in different spheres, these spheres are best allocated correctly to each gender. If she has stewardship of household finances, she is not free to 'cream off' household money to buy herself some jewelry - she is accountable to you, and every so often you insist on sitting down together to review the 'books', during which time she takes responsibility for her 'stewardship' as 'caretaker' of household funds. You tend to be the 'head' of the relationship as opposed to its 'heart', so your strengths will tend to be goal setting, analysis and so on.

The domestic roles that have to be allocated include:

Home Finances

Garden Maintenance

Cooking, washing dishes and so on

Laundry - washing and ironing

Looking after the children – and when

Shopping

Home maintenance and D.I.Y.

Cleaning, dusting and window cleaning

Decorating

The more you go into details – who, what, when, how often and so on, the better.

'Emotional intelligence' requires emotional understanding and an emotional response

The following situation was played out on three or four occasions over the years between my mother and father. It would be a Saturday night and my father would be lying on the sofa after an evening meal, half watching the television. After a while, my mother would ask:

> 'Are we going out then?' [Child – given away by tone of voice]

My father would say something like:

> 'I'm not overly bothered, I'm happy watching T.V.' [Adult]

My mother would fold her arms and indignantly say:

> 'I knew it! I knew you didn't want to go out!' [Frustrated Child]

Father would prop himself up and say something like:

> 'Well, if you want to go out then we'll go out. I'll get ready.' [Adult]

Instantly my mother would defiantly respond:

> 'Oh no! I don't want to go out when you are not really bothered!' [Child]

Father would sink back onto the sofa again. My mother, even more indignantly, would declare:

> 'See! I *knew* you didn't want to go out!' [Child]

Father would now sit up and say:

> 'O.K. I'll get ready. We'll go out.' [Adult]

Mother would reply:

> 'Oh no! You're not really bothered - I don't want to go out!' [Child]

Father would sink back onto the sofa again [Adult] and there would be a sullen silence from my mother [Child] for an hour or so. As I've said before:

'There's logic here Captain, but not as we know it'

There is an *appearance* of logic and she even uses *cognitive language*, but my mother's logic and cognition is underpinned by her emotions, such that her thoughts are distorted or even completely hijacked.

Your girlfriend's emotions may be no stronger than yours – but she is more in touch with and more influenced by them. In the example above, you may think that her question 'Are we going out tonight' is a *logical* question and that she is seeking an *evaluative opinion*. In fact, it is an *emotional* statement: 'I *feel like* going out tonight and I *need* you with me because I *feel* alone and insecure going out on my own' and the behavior and attitude of females in Child are often based on their 'gut reaction'.

You will be confronted with 'emotional intelligence' again and again, so let's look at it more closely.

In this dispute about whether to go out or not - the strong male [Parent] response is to get her [Child] to state clearly what she wants:

> F: 'Are we going out then?' [Child - I am *feeling* impatient because time is slipping by and I would *love* to go out.]

> M: 'Do *you* want to go out?' [Parent/Adult]

Or:

> M: 'Do *you feel* like going out?' [Adult checking her emotional needs at this moment]

She either:

a) Wants to speculate [Adult] so you let her; or,

b) She already has an emotional need or desire [Child], so you get her to state it clearly.

Always get her to state clearly

what she wants

If she throws the question back at you, or if she hesitates, or is vague, take a clear lead immediately [Parent] and reply:

> M: 'If you're asking *me* whether *I* want to go out, the answer is No!' [Authoritarian Parent]

Remember - always adopt Parent position in response to her Child. If her behavior or attitude is unacceptable, remove your humor to adopt your more authoritarian or disciplinarian Parental approach.

Your response is a simple 'No' – no reasons or explanations. Keep things brief or vague. If she asks whether you are going to see her tonight and you are out with your mates, you reply:

'I'm out'

As opposed to:

'I'm out with my friends'

If you give explanations and reasons, you move from being one up Parent to the one down position of Adult or even two down position of Child. She becomes 'superior' Parent and your explanations give her ammunition and a set of targets to home in on and demolish –

'So, you'd rather see your friends instead of me.'

This is either [Child not getting the attention she wants] or [Parent trying to set the agenda]. Either way, she demands further explanations. **These things are none of her business.** Your decision 'No' is enough [Parent].

If she wants to go out and you want to stay in you can reply with an *emotive response*:

' I don't *want* to.'

Or:

'I *feel* like staying in'. [Parent controlled use of Child emotional response].

If she still carries on, you can be vague:

'I *don't know why* I want to stay in, I just *feel* like staying in.' [Parent controlled use of Child emotional response].

Emotive statements like this serve two functions:

> They connect with her emotional level - you are talking language that she is familiar with, especially in Child

> No further explanation is required - emotional statements are an end in themselves - a statement of fact she can't disagree with - so they form the bottom line.

The statement: 'I *feel* sad' is a fact. *You* may not feel sad but *I* do. If other people tell you that you 'don't feel sad', 'should not' feel sad or that going out will make you feel happier, or that you 'should' pull yourself together, these are all [Parent] attempts to get you to do what they want you to do. The vague emotional statement: 'I don't know why I feel sad, I just do' dismisses thought, emphasizes emotions and removes both specific targets and any ammunition for them to use against you. It says in effect: 'I feel sad - end of story - you know how it feels and you can't deny how I feel - you may not like it - but that's the way it is.'

> # Give no explanations for your
>
> # opinions and actions

Here's another example: A date has been arranged following a flurry of flirting, but she's had time to *think* a little ['Emotional intelligence'] and starts to *worry* that she'll be thought of as being 'easy' or a 'tart' [Child]. So she texts or phones you -

F: 'I hope you don't think I do this sort of thing all the time'

This is code for: 'I don't want to **feel** that I'm a tart.' 'I don't want to **feel** that other people think or feel I'm a tart '.

The *apparently* cognitive statement:

'I hope you don't *think* I do this sort of thing all the time' is really an *emotional* **statement**: 'I'm feeling like a bit of a tart right now and need reassurance that I'm not a tart and that you don't feel I'm a tart either.' [Child]

The rational, weak response would be to reply to her text immediately and rationally [Adult], placing you one down right away, as if you are running after her to make sure that her desires are satisfied. Worse still, you would reply with something *unemotional and logical* [Adult] such as -

M: 'No, I don't **think** you are like that at all'. [Adult]

Don't respond to her Child in your Adult. Delay your reply by an hour or two [Parent] to show that you are not at her beck and call and to establish your command of the situation [Self-confident Parent]. The text that you send later may say something like:

M: 'What we have is the start of something special'.
[Integrated Parent/Adult accessing her passionate Child]

You calculate [Adult] to give her a passionate response [Child] that addresses her emotions. You suggest that she is special and that the relationship *feels* special and passionate. This is a calculated, perhaps even a cynical

Parent/Adult tactic to appeal to her Child vanity as someone who is the center of your attention. The use of text has given you control over the timing of your response [Parent], and given you time to think [Adult] of an appropriate emotional response [Child]. [Integrated Male response]

If she has a tantrum, starts pleading, or becomes rebellious [Child], you always respond with humorless authoritarian, disciplinarian Parent. But you don't want to kill her passion by overly criticizing her Child - you want to feed the positive aspects of her Child position. So you pander to her Child a little, to draw out and reassure her Child, so as to encourage her passion. But tantrums, foot stamping, rebelling, finger – wagging, bossiness, being defiant and so on are not acceptable aspects of her Child as far as you are concerned [Adult. Boundary setting]. So by *controlled* expressions of your own passion [Integrated Parent/Adult/Child]; by rewarding her *acceptable* Child behaviors and attitudes with warmth, closeness and attention; and by discouraging her unacceptable Child behaviors and attitudes through the withdrawal deterrents, you can draw out her vibrant Child.

Passion and romance

His idea of 'eating out' is sending me to the chip shop to bring home fish and chips so we can eat them in the back garden'

Most males don't have much idea when it comes to romance and passion. Sending texts to your mates during a romantic meal is not good - she might leave and then text you to pay for the meal. Romance and passion are skills you need to learn. Being passionate about everything and using romantic, poetic language as well as humor, all involve you expressing your inner Child – but in a controlled way – because for many males, getting in touch with inner Child means 'play' rather than 'romance'.

For example, you don't see your girlfriend because you are out with your mates. Next day, you meet up with your girlfriend and she says:

F: 'Did you see/enjoy meeting your friends?'

This could be an Adult logical inquiry, or it could be 'emotional intelligence' where her Child is saying 'I *felt* lonely without you, I hope *you feel* the same, I *need* you and *I hope you need me* because I want to *feel* as though we *belong*' or it could even be, 'I *feel* resentful of you seeing your friends because they take you and your attention *away from me*. I *crave* your attention and if you were *happy* without me last night then that makes me *feel* even worse.'

A weak / logical [Adult] response might be:

M: 'Yes, I had a good time but I thought about you a lot, you're the best'. [Adult]

You were probably in Child when you were with your friends

- it was all about *playing*. When your girlfriend calls and reminds you of the previous night, your thoughts will be about *playtime*. Today you're in Adult, and *conclude* that you'd better say you were *thinking* about her - even if you weren't - so you say, 'I *thought* about you a lot', and then you lamely add - 'you're the best'. Because you are in cognitive, analytical Adult it means that your response is bland and that it lacks passion. ***It does not connect with her emotional sphere***.

A more poetic, romantic, passionate, emotional response would be something like:

> F: 'Did you see/enjoy meeting your friends?'

> M: 'Yes, but they were like stars fading in the dawn – It's you that forms my bright sun in the heavens'. [Integrated Parent/Adult/Child].

Although this response seems to be emotional [Child], you may have thought it up beforehand [Adult] and are now using it in a calculated way [Parent/Adult] to increase her passion, her sense of belonging and her readiness to be bedded. This more poetic, romantic, passionate *emotive* language readily connects with *her* emotions. But it requires you to shift your Child away from its natural tendency towards 'play' to focus instead on 'romance'.

Men are passionate about life

(And Football!)

Male and female passion

Males are passionate about *ideas and technology* - politics, theology, philosophy, mechanical engineering, Mars landing craft, Steam locomotives, Airplanes, Science fiction or computer science. Solving technical problems - fixing the car engine - can send males into raptures. But these subjects make females bored because they are not passionate about ideas or technology. Worse still, when you are passionate about such themes, she *feels* as though your attention is being taken away from her. The one thing she wants is your attention on her [Child].

Don't talk much to females about

ideas or technical subjects

Passion about your career

A male who is focused on his career is ambitious and passionate about his work. Since childhood, he may have devoted much of his life to learning and developing his skills at his profession. If he is a skilled piano player, he may have started piano lessons when he was five or six years old. He is serious about his profession to the point of not drinking alcohol at all if it interferes with his career or takes the edge off his skills. Although his girlfriend may constantly offer him alcoholic drinks, especially if she drinks herself, he will almost certainly refuse every time.

F: 'Don't you like Martini?' [Adult]

M: 'Not much.' [Adult]

F: 'They *are* an acquired taste.' [Parent]

M: 'I don't have much time for acquired taste'. [Parent]

He has a laser-like focus on the goals that he has set for himself in his career. Females are attracted to his passion and single-minded dedication – but often, they want *themselves* to be the exclusive object of his passion and dedication. They see his passion and want to feel the experience of being on the receiving end of it. She may see his career as a rival, because it draws his passions away from her and so she may be as resentful of his career as she would be of another female he was having an affair with. She may see him as being 'married to his job'. As one wife once said to her violinist husband: 'I don't want to play second fiddle to your violin!'

In small talk she may try to draw him away from his focus on his career to try and find some other way of engaging and turning his passion to her.

F: 'What do you do for fun?' [Adult]

M: 'I play the violin' [For 'violin' read passionate career/hobby] [Adult]

F: 'Is that all that you do, play the violin?' [Parent]

M: 'Almost.' [Parent]

F: 'Hobbies? Pleasure?'

M: 'They're in the violin for me.' [Adult]

F: 'Girls?'

M: 'A few'. [Adult]

F: 'That's all?'

M: 'That's all!' [Parent]

She will eventually complain that she is not getting enough attention - his job gets more of his time than she does. His arguments that she knew how important his career was to him [Adult], won't carry much weight. What *she* saw was his *passion*, not his career, hobby or goals.

In this situation you have to make a choice. She wants you entirely on her own terms. You have to decide whether to sacrifice your career/hobby goals to her needs, or whether to remain uncompromising concerning your career/hobby aims. Lack of compromise is the manly approach – but she may find this unacceptable and in effect, lose you because of her insistent demands, distractions and criticisms.

Poetry

Writing poetry about her can be a great way to make a connection with her emotions. It doesn't even have to rhyme - it just makes use of lyrical, romantic language - this is the aspect that connects with her. Key words and themes in poetry include:

Adornment, Beauty, Bringing forth life, Closeness, Comfort, Communication, Communion, Continuity, Dancing, Delicate, Desire, Embrace, Emergence, Emotions, Erotic, Eruption, Essence, Excitement, Expansiveness, Feelings, Fellowship, Fertile, Fruit, Gentleness, Goddess, Growth, Help, Hypnotic, Inclusion, Inner Depths, Invitation, Laughter, Lovemaking, Lushness, Abandonment of thought, Helping you to forget, Play, Music, Nakedness, Natural cycles, Nearness, Nurture, Passion, Peace, Present Reality, Princess, Proximity, Pulsating, Quietness, Reaching your Heart or the Core of your Being, Receptivity, Relationships, Giving you Respite and Rest, Rhythms, Giving you satisfaction, Seasons, Senses, Sensuousness, Giving you strength, Support, Surrender, Swaying, Sweet Fragrance, Swirling, Tenderness, Union, Unrelenting, Voluptuousness, Warmth, Working together.

These words and phrases may seem strange to you because you operate in a rational, analytical, task orientated [Adult] way - cold, boring and nerdish to females – so you look like an 'anorak' to her.

You may have to work hard at giving her attention because you are *task* orientated – you have busy schedules and things to do to meet your goals, aims, targets and plans. But you really do have to make time in your busy schedules to attend to her emotions, feelings and passions.

Other romantic / emotional gestures include buying her flowers because of who she is, cooking a romantic meal for two and so on.

Warning!

Because this is strange to you, you may fall into the trap of arousing her *suspicion*. Buying her flowers for no obvious reason may arouse her suspicion that you feel guilty about something - like having an affair. 'He's never done this before', 'I am not really worth it', 'I've done nothing to deserve it', 'It's not a special occasion, he must feel guilty'. Responses like this have to be dealt with quickly and without humor.

> M: 'I bought you flowers/chocolates because I (love/appreciate) you. If this is how you react I won't bother again and I'll give the flowers/chocolates to someone who *will* appreciate them!' [Parent]

Pick up the flowers/chocolates and leave for a while. [Male disciplinary Parent, Withdrawal of humor, gift and self]. Unless of course she is suitably apologetic, in which case you stay.

Here's an example of the romantic/poetic approach in an online chat room: A female asks males what would they give her to impress her on a first date. One guy suggests a box of chocolates; another guy suggests flowers. As more males reply they try to outdo one another in the size and expense of their 'gifts' - a meal, a day out, a visit to theatre and so on. Finally one guy says; 'I'll give you my heart'. He's the one she chooses.

This use of poetry and romance is an aspect of your Child. As I have said, the usual inclination of your Child is to play: go to the pub and get pissed, go to a football match with your mates, spend hours on a Play Station games console, or watch the Hulk kicking shit out of Loki. There is nothing wrong with appropriate play, but you need to broaden your appreciation of your Child and encourage other aspects of it, such as romance and poetry. Reading the romantic poets can be one way of getting in touch with the passion that romance contains.

Here's an example of simple use of romance. Your girlfriend is standing on some stepladders:

>F: 'What if I fall?'

>M: ' I'll let you fall into my arms.'

If you get an 'Ahhhh!' from any females standing nearby, you have just scored one point on the female reward system.

Passion tip

Lightly placing your hand on your girlfriend's throat as you lean forward to kiss her is an effective display of passion, especially if she is talking too much, or is in an argument with you. It has a subtle effect, as if you are taking charge to stop the flow of words and the needless sound from her mouth to make room for passion.

'Emotional intelligence' and decision-making

Here's a classic situation: You're in the women's clothes section of a department store and your girlfriend holds up two dresses, a red one and a black one and says:

F: 'Which do you prefer?'

Straight away you sense you are caught in a trap. This could be a logical inquiry [Adult] or an example of 'emotional intelligence' using cognitive words and phrases [Child].

A weak male remains in cognitive mode [Adult] and points to one of the dresses and says:

M: 'That one.' [Adult]

F: 'What's wrong with the other one?'

He's fallen into the trap and entered the Dark Continent; somehow he has picked the wrong dress and missed something - somewhere along the line he was given a hint that he should have picked the other one. Confused and still in cognitive mode, he struggles to come up with *reasons*

[Adult] for not picking the dress that she seems to prefer. Thrown off course and lost in the emotional labyrinth, he gives up and says -

> M: 'I don't *know*.' [Exasperated Adult]

Or:

> M: 'Either is fine.' [Surrendering Adult]

Or:

> M: 'I don't *mind* - whichever one you like'. [Abdicating Adult]

She may then launch into verbal abuse -

> F: 'That's the trouble: you don't care about anything' [Critical Parent or Angry Child according to tone of voice]

Or:

> F: 'Call yourself a man? You can't make a decision about anything.' [Critical Parent]

If you learn to correctly recognise that her question is an *emotional* one rather than a logical one, then

You are released from having to find any sort of logical solution

Believe it or not, the pressure is off.

You don't always have

to find solutions

Emotional questions free you from the burden of trying to find a cognitive, logical solution.

So how **do** you respond to this question?

It doesn't matter which dress you choose but it *is* important to select one or the other. In making a decision you seem to be in command, to be decisive and authoritative [Parent]. So you select a dress - any dress - it doesn't matter.

Don't even try to guess what she's feeling, and don't take any notice of any hints she seems to give you. *All of these are irrelevant.*

When you have made your choice, whatever it is, she will probably question your decision - 'What's wrong with this other one?' **This is another *emotional* question**, so you are still under no pressure to logically explain your choice. Because it's an emotional question, you respond using emotional language –

> F: 'What's wrong with the other one?'

> M: 'Nothing. I'm just *intuitively drawn* to that one'

Or:

> M: ' Nothing. I just *feel* that one is best'

Or:

M: ' Nothing. It's just a *gut feeling* that I prefer that one'

By referring to your 'intuition' or 'gut feeling', no further explanation can be given - your 'intuition' is the bottom line - you may even say:

M: *'I don't know* - I just intuitively *feel* that....'. No reasons given. [Parent]

Her responses such as: 'That's the trouble: you don't care about anything', or 'Call yourself a man? You can't make a decision about anything' arise from Parent. Males turn sheepish and mumble a vague reply, but if you do this, she's successfully put you into Child and you are two down. Stay in Parent, remove any humor to allow your Authoritarian or Disciplinarian Parent to respond:

M: 'I was trying to give you my preference. Don't ask me again if that's your attitude.' [Disciplinarian Parent]

Here's another common example:

F: 'Am I fat?'

Or:

F: 'Do I look fat in this?'

This is an *emotional* statement that has an appearance of logical inquiry. She *feels* fat and this will make her *feel* unhappy; so one approach is to by-pass the question completely:

M: 'You don't look very happy.' [Integrated Parent/Adult]

'Emotional intelligence': Not giving her time to think

Don't give her room to think, or options to evaluate, analyse and make a decision about. Here is an example of making the mistake of giving her space to think:

M: 'There's a good live band on at the club next Thursday. Shall we go?'

F: 'Maybe'.

This has got him nowhere at all. Zilch. Better to say:

M: 'There's a good live band on at the club next Thursday. Let's go see them' [Parent].

You take the lead and suggest the decision. She's still free to say yes or no. If she says 'Maybe' *then you can decide on her behalf that she is **not** going.*

M: 'If you're not bothered I'll find someone else who *is* interested.' [Disciplinary Parent using Withdrawal deterrent and threat of further deterrent]

Or at least:

M: 'If you're not interested, forget it – I'm going anyway - see you later.' [Disciplinary Parent using Withdrawal Deterrent]

This is the tactic of **'Hidden Parental Guidance'**. If there are three or four options and a decision is required, then if *you* have a preference you suggest it in the form of a question. For example, both a new 'chick flick' as well as the latest Bond film are showing at the cinema. You fancy Jimmy Bond, so you say:

M: 'The latest Bond movie is showing this week - let's go see it.' [Integrated Parent/Adult/Child].

You don't mention the 'chick flick' option at all. The tactic of 'Hidden Parental Guidance' means that you move her the way *you* want to go. She has three options –

'Yes',

'No' or

F: 'I'd rather see [the chick flick].' [Integrated Adult/Child]

(She has seen for herself that the 'chick flick' is showing). In which case *you* can say 'Yes' or 'No' [Adult] without reasons [Parent] but your 'gut feeling' is that you would enjoy Jimmy Bond better. [Parent. Emotional response]

Use your 'Unseen Parental Guiding Hand'

to help her make the right decision –

the decision that you want

Unspoken hints and implications

Your girlfriend will often use *indirect* forms of communication - hints, implications, body language, tone of voice and so on - to seemingly to give you hints about what she wants. If she wants something (or someone), she goes after it (or them) by using hidden and round about pathways – she won't use the shortest or most obvious path. If she follows the shortest route, other females will gossip about her.

Here's what I mean: You are both relaxing at home when she says:

> F: 'Oh dear! I have to pick the children up. I guess I'll have to get the bus.'

She couples this with pleading eyes, and/or a pitiful, sad or questioning tone of voice [Child].

You may easily think that she means that she wants you to give her a lift in the car to pick up the children. You make the offer and she takes you up on it. Later, you end up in an argument over the remote control and you mention that you did her a favor earlier by giving her a lift in your car. She completely dismisses this and says she never asked you for a lift; or she says: '*You* chose to offer'.

If you fall into this trap there is still time to rescue yourself and establish the Boundary line:

> F: '*You* chose to offer, I never asked you for a lift.' (Score zero on the female reward system)

> M: Yes. I chose to offer you a lift because I was trying to help you. But I won't do it again.'. [Integrated authoritarian/disciplinarian Parent and Adult using Withdrawal Deterrent and resetting Boundaries, Child

humor withdrawn]

Never try to mind read what she wants - Always get her to say clearly and openly what she wants

It's not your responsibility to try and second-guess what's in her emotional mind. Rather, it's *her* responsibility to say clearly what she wants [Adult].

With this in mind, the exchange can now look like this:

F: 'Oh dear! I have to pick the children up. I guess I'll have to get the bus.'

What she *says* is an Adult statement of fact, but her pleading eyes and pitiful, sad or questioning tone of voice all indicate that she is in Child and that she seems to be giving you hints that she wants you to give her a lift in your car.

M: 'O.K. I'll see you later' [Parent]

You respond in Parent to her female Childish hints – you give no reasons and no explanations. You ignore the tone of voice and body language and respond to what she actually says. In other words

You ignore all her hints and implications

She may try again:

F: 'I'll have to dash – I'm running late' [Female Adult statement with female Childish hints – a lift in your car would be quicker]

M: 'O.K.' [Parent]

You continue to ignore her hints. Then she changes her approach:

F: 'Actually, could you give me a lift?' [Adult]

She finally states clearly what she wants by moving fully to Adult and letting go of her unspoken Childish hints.

M: 'Of course I can'. [Immediate move to Adult in response]

When she asks openly

and directly, always try

to do what she asks,

if **her request is reasonable**

Here's another example:

You are relaxing at home when you get an unasked for text message from your girlfriend:

> F: 'I am on the bus.'

This seems to be so meaningless to you that you think that there must be something extra - a suggestion hidden here somewhere. Perhaps this is a hint to 'Get the house tidy', or 'Start making tea' e.t.c.. 'I am on the bus' is ambiguous to you because it seems to have no real purpose, especially since you are expecting her to come home about this time anyway.

If your girlfriend tends mainly to be in Child, you know that she often uses hidden paths – it's happened before when she asked questions like: 'Which set of cushions do you prefer?' So 'I am on the bus' could very well carry hidden meanings and traps that you can't see. You begin to think 'What now?' - there *must* be some underlying reason and purpose for her message. So you begin to add hidden meanings of your own to what she has said, such as 'I am being told to tidy up', or 'I should come away from the computer/games machine now'. When you add your own meanings onto what she has said, you *project* your own feelings, doubts, anxieties or guilt onto the empty spaces that seem to fill her message. Then, in addition, you displace the unsettling negative qualities that you feel in yourself, such as guilt about untidiness or too much time spent on the computer, onto her - *she* is always nagging you to get the house tidy, and she always moans about you spending too much time on the games console.

In fact it may actually be that she has

only sent the text: 'I am on the bus'

How do you deal with this? You do the same as in the previous example: you ignore any hints – and you only pay attention to what is actually said. There are only two real responses to such unasked for texts:

M: 'Great' [Adult]

Or:

No response [Parent]

A lack of response means that you don't give her the emotional connection that she may be seeking. 'I am on the bus' may be an example of 'emotional intelligence' in which she is expressing her *need* to belong [Child]. But it is not your responsibility to second guess whether this is the case or not - she has to **say** what she wants: 'I am on the bus. Missed you. Looking forward to seeing you soon.' So:

Ignore anything you *think* or *feel* she is saying but which she hasn't *actually* said

'Emotional intelligence' and leading questions

Your girlfriend may use leading questions or statements that seem to guide you to an answer she seems to require. The 'leading question tactic' is another variation of the 'hints and implications' strategy that we have just looked at.

But, in another prime example of 'emotional intelligence', the answer that she may actually want will be the *very opposite* of what she is directing you to. This is a minefield of confusion.

When she communicates like this, is it any wonder that males sometimes conclude that when she says 'No' she really means 'Yes'. However, your strategy is simple. It is the same as your response to hints and implications:

Ignore all the leading hints of direction

in her questions and statements

Here's an example.

You get a text message as part of arranging a date. She says:

> F: 'I hope you behave yourself tonight.'

She could be any position - Parent, Adult or Child.

You may think that she is hinting that she wants you to be on your best behavior - seeing her message as a straightforward Adult statement where she says what she means. **Actually she is stating the exact opposite**, as we shall see in a moment.

Make a face value Adult interpretation of her statement and **you reverse the true situation**. Actually she is speaking **emotionally** - her *desire* is for you to **misbehave** [Child]. But it is unacceptable for her to say this openly – if she did, she would have to face the internal criticism of her own Adult and Parent, making her feel disapproval and conflict inside. So **she says the opposite of what she really wants** - a statement that's acceptable to her Critical Parent and Adult. She is actually making hints, hoping that you will pick up on what she *really* means and take the initiative so that she can avoid feeling guilty. Keep that length of string handy for the labyrinthine maze that you are entering so that you can find your way back to sanity.

There are two options for your reply to this text -

Option 1 -

> M: 'I always behave myself – I'm very good - even when I'm bad I'm good.' [Integrated Parent with Child humor]

You deal with her question in a humorous way [Child] that implies the opposite of what *you* are saying - you return her tactic back to her - and in doing so, by using humor you connect with her emotions [Child].

Option 2 -

> M: 'No. I don't think I *can* behave myself. I'll just behave as I normally do.' [Integrated Parent/Adult/Child]

This is exactly the opposite strategy to Option 1, but just as effective. You honestly declare [Adult] your intention to not to change [Parent] even if that means misbehaving [Child]. This can be invaluable later if arguments arise because you can remind her that you were quite up front and honest [Adult].

Interestingly her reaction to option 2 was:

> F: 'Good. I don't like weak men or wimps'. [Child] (Message - I feel that well-behaved men are weak and wimps)

And this confirms the *implied misdirection* of her question.

Testing times

If ever your girlfriend says 'I was just testing' it is evidence that she has uttered a misdirection or hint. When it comes to indirect and leading statements, the ultimate is when she says:

F: 'Can't you take a hint?'

I have suggested that your answer to this is

M: 'No'

Who on earth can second-guess what is going on in a female's mind? If she wants to create a labyrinth then that's fine - she can find her own way in and out of it. If she wants a mind-reader she can go to a clairvoyant. You - you are not even going to go there.

F: 'Can't you take a hint?'

M: 'No. Say what you mean.' [Parent/Adult - Child humor withdrawn]

Time for a Test!

To try and find out what kind of person you are, females will 'test' you. Here's why - if she *openly* asks you, 'Are you an honest man?' you will say 'Yes, of course I am'. Asking straightforward questions like this will not get her anywhere. She doesn't know whether you are lying or not. So she has to use **indirect** approaches to see if she can catch you out and find out what sort of male you *really* are.

The good news is –

If she's testing you – she's interested in you

So, since we are looking at her indirect approaches and hints, I will briefly look at some strategies she may use.

Female tests, Male tactics

1) Female provocation

Two guys invite a female work colleague to have a meal break with them following some earlier joking and flirting, but she makes excuses. You could move on to the next female since this one has not shown much evidence in the way of doing as she is told. However, later on, she makes comments and starts verbal games as a way of provoking reactions from the two guys who plan more banter:

> 1st Male to Female: 'I'm very surprised you refused an invitation to have a meal with two males.' (Note that he uses the word 'male' here instead of 'men', thus avoiding giving her the chance to say that she can't see any men, or some such put down).

> F: 'You wouldn't pay for breakfast anyway.' [Female testing]

> 1st Male [Weak response] 'You didn't give us a chance to offer!'

> 2nd Male [Strong response] 'I wouldn't have paid for *your* breakfast anyway.' [Parent]

A female may provoke you for a number of reasons.

a) Boredom – the last thing she'll put up with.

b) She may desire a more passionate response. She may sense that you are passionate, but you are passionate about your career or your hobby - about *things* rather than *her*. As a result she may doubt her own attractiveness or be uncertain of your attraction to her.

c) She may use provocation as a **test**. *She will test any male she is interested in to determine how manly he is.* How quickly will he stand up to her provocative behavior and assert his manhood? Is he a weak male who will too easily give in to her demands?

Her provocative behavior may include:

Doing or saying outrageous things

Doing or saying things she knows you will hate

Doing things that hinder your plans

Getting you to do trivial or embarrassing tasks

2) **Female displays of authority**

F: 'Put the tray over there, there's a good boy.' [Female Parent]

In this case you put the tray anywhere but where she asked for it to be put. Or, for example, she may provoke a reaction by returning a trolley to the work area and leaving it where it will cause an obvious obstruction. In this case, you call her name, beckon her towards you and whisper in her ear:

M: 'Put the trolley back where you got it from, there's a good girl.' [Parent]

Or:

M: 'You've left the trolley in the wrong place sweetheart.' [Male Parent talking to her like a Child]

Or:

M: 'You're being a very naughty girl! You're asking for a smacked bottom.' [Parent]

Or:

M: Naughty girl! No treats for you tonight.' [Parent]

If she does as she is told and returns the trolley to its proper place:

M: 'Good girl! Give yourself a chocolate/treat!' [Parent]

3) Unasked for advice

If a female sees a married male work colleague getting involved in flirtatious behavior with a female co-worker, she may say something like:

F: 'Be careful! She's a strong woman and you're married!' [Parent]

But males don't make this kind of comment to other males. They are more likely to laughingly say: 'Ohh!

Wait till your wife finds out!' Males tend not to use phrases such as 'Be careful'; 'Watch out'; 'You need to behave yourself'; or 'Grow up'.

If the flirtatious male had approached the critical female and *asked* for her advice, things would be completely different:

> M: 'What do you think about me and Liz flirting?' [Adult]

> F: 'I think you should be careful. She's a strong woman and you're married.' [Adult]

This is fine because the male has *asked* her for her comments. But you always rebuff [Parent] *unasked* for advice with humor [Child].

> F: 'Be careful! She's a strong woman and you're married!' [Parent]

> M: 'Yes mother!' [Parent with humor]

4) Criticism

If you are faced with criticism from a female in her Critical Parent role, use the verbal technique of 'Fogging' that I described earlier. This approach helps you to avoid the **Male Vanity Trap** because you do **not** respond to her criticism by pushing forward your own positive qualities.

There is an example of this approach in the classic 1940's movie 'The Big Sleep':

> F: 'I don't like your manners!' [Parent]

M: 'And I'm not crazy about yours. I don't mind if you don't like my manners. I don't like them myself. They are pretty bad. I grieve over them on long winter evenings.' [Parent with humor]

5) **Female challenges to your manhood**

This is when females challenge you with a dare - like contests of strength or endurance – who can make the highest dive into the water; who can be the most rebellious or disobedient and take the greatest punishment with the least complaining. Any failure on your part to take up such her challenge carries with it an implication that you are weak and immature – that you are not a man. But this may also be her verdict if you accept the challenge and then fail. The worst-case scenario is that she takes the challenge herself and beats you.

Females may challenge you to a dare and trick you by playing dishonestly. For example, in the 'who can be the most rebellious and take the greatest punishment' challenge, she may change the rules so that she avoids punishment altogether and then mocks you for making the most noise when you were punished.

Remember - *you* set your own agenda – she doesn't set your agenda for you. You are not going to climb that forty-foot high chimney to adjust the T.V. antenna just because she has decided it needs doing and that she can manipulate you into doing it by equating this task with your manhood.

In such cases it's best to be direct:

> M: 'I decide if and when and I attend to the T.V. antenna, not you. And I've decided I'm not doing it. [Parent, Boundary Setting]

6) 'What kind of woman do you like?'

Females often ask this question and the worst answer that you can give is something like:

> M: 'A woman like you'.

Disinterest and detachment are key approaches you can try, or alternatively, answer her in such a way that you don't really answer her at all.

For example – she is feisty and you make a comment:

> M: 'Ah! A willful woman!'

> F: 'Could you love a willful woman? [Can you love *me*?]

> M: 'During passing moments.'

> F: 'But not forever?'

> M: 'Who speaks of 'forever' in the same breath as love?' [Laugh or Wink with smile]

> F: 'If you can't love a willful woman, who *can* you love?'

[How can I present myself to you so that you will love *me*?]

M: 'A soft gentle woman who would be a pillow for my head but leave my heart free.'

F: 'You would soon get tired and bored of her softness.' [I don't want to be submissive]

M: 'Then I'd throw her on one side. Pillows are cheap and easily found.' [Detached disinterest]

F: 'Why are you afraid of love?

M: 'Why does the stallion fear the spur?

Remember this principle:

A woman is just for Christmas!

'Emotional intelligence' and faulty logic

Because her thoughts and reasoning processes are underpinned by her emotions, her conclusions are often faulty, or in effect non-logical. Here is what I mean -

You finished a fairly long-term relationship a few months ago and you have recently been seeing another girlfriend. But after a few weeks you have decided to end this new relationship. Hurt and angry, your rejected new girlfriend decides to contact your previous ex-girlfriend to say what a bastard you are.

Most males would assume that her purpose is to get

revenge on you in some way. But the reason that she contacts your previous girlfriend is an emotional one: feeling rejected and isolated, she needs to regain her felt-sense of belonging and she needs empathy. Who is most likely to empathize with how she feels? Your previous ex-girlfriend, because she has gone through the same experience and will have felt the same emotions, so she can empathize best.

Males look for **logical** reasons for people's actions - but female 'emotional intelligence' has **emotional reasons** that influence her behavior, and her emotions don't follow cognitive logic.

Thus this situation requires no response from you at all.

> Female 'logic' follows hidden
>
> emotional rules, so you
>
> can't possibly understand it

'Emotional intelligence' and the blame game

You are on your way to the airport for a holiday with your girlfriend and as you approach the airport she asks -

> F: 'Did you bring the passports?'

This could be any position - Parent, Adult or Child. Non-verbal cues may help you to decide which position she is in. It could be Parent checking up that you've done everything you were supposed to. It could be a genuine, logical, straightforward Adult inquiry. It could be anxious Child worrying whether you both have your passports or not.

M: 'No, you said you were bringing them' [Adult]

F: 'Do I have to do *everything*?' [Child. All or nothing thinking]

She had agreed to take responsibility for this task [Adult] but has failed to complete it - she is at fault. Her 'emotional intelligence' means that she feels 'upset' and 'annoyed' [Child] *at herself* because with all the other things that she had to do (just as *you* had other things to do as well), she has forgotten to bring the passports. Feeling 'overwhelmed' at all the things she had to do, in 'exasperation' she declares: 'Do I have to do *everything*?' - *implying* that the forgotten passports are somehow *your* fault. By projecting her guilt and failure onto you, she relieves her own negative feelings about herself. This is not about logic; it is about her getting relief from her negative emotions.

You can correct her faulty logic by saying -

> M: 'No, you don't have to do *everything* but you *did* take responsibility for bringing the passports.' [Integrated Parent/Adult - Child humor withdrawn]

She *should* be upset and angry - with herself and her failure to bring the passports. You can't allow her to project the emotional consequences of her actions or failure to act [Child] on to *you* - she must take accountability [Adult] for her own actions and her emotions.

Females use projection as a defense tactic. Phrases like 'Do I have to do everything?', 'Look what you made me do!'; or 'I forgot - that's your fault!' - are all examples of your girlfriend projecting her own guilt or sense of failure onto someone else, usually *you*. Girlfriends in Child frequently project like this – like a little child she wants to get involved in everything, but when things go wrong, the Child in her is quick to blame anyone or anything else. She passes the buck and doesn't want to take responsibility. As far as she is concerned, such responsibility is always 'out there' with something or someone else. You can't let this happen - she *must* take responsibility for her actions; after all, she really is grown up now.

Always make her take responsibility for her actions - or lack of them

'Emotional intelligence': More examples

Females often feel that their own personal interests are the same as the interests of her wider family, or an even wider circle of people.

Your female partner may phone or text:

> F: 'The kids want to see you.'

Or:

> F: 'The kids are missing you.'

In Adult you will tend to take such statements at face value. But this may be another **emotional statement** that means:

> 'I am missing you because I don't have a babysitter and I want to go out'.

She makes her *personal* desire the same as that of the kids, but there is also emotional blackmail here. She is blatantly using emotions (hers, the kids and yours) to try to get her own way [Child]. She is trying to drag you into the emotional swamp - to make you feel guilty - by 'tugging at your heartstrings'. Her tactic of emotional blackmail will be revealed more fully if it fails. She will step up her emotions to the next degree in her attempt to try and press the right buttons to get the response she wants. Such steps include: anger/threats, tears/sobbing, pleading and depression. If you don't respond or you say you're busy, she may reply:

> F: 'You'll end up on your own - lonely and eaten up by bitterness with no one to love or care for you!' [Angry Child].

She may go through a whole range of emotional tactics to try to make you feel guilty - from rage, to self-pity, to tears, to bitterness, to forgiveness – anything to find the emotional 'button' that will get you to do what she wants.

Cool, logical detachment is the order of the day as far as you can manage it [Adult].

> When she shows emotionally charged, unacceptable behavior, stay as emotionally detached as you can

Pre-empting emotional situations

It can be useful to pre-empt emotional situations by getting her to express her own emotional opinion before you say what *you* think.

A classic example is the hairdressers - always an emotional situation. Your girlfriend arrives home from the hairdressers and thinking you are being complimentary by noticing and acknowledging this fact at all, you say:

> M: 'Hi honey. Been to the hairdressers? Your hair looks lovely.' [Integrated Adult/Child]

She then bursts into tears sobbing about what a disaster the hairdresser has made of her hair - and *you* think it looks good. [Child]

The technique here is to avoid all eye contact and get her to express *her* feelings *first*. As soon as she is opening the front door, go into another room, or go upstairs, or bury your head in a cupboard, or the fridge and then, whilst **not looking at her** you call out -

> M: 'Hi honey. Been to the hairdressers? How do you *feel*?'

You've not seen her hair so you can't comment. As soon as she gives her response, you can **agree with it - whatever it is**. [Fogging]

> F: 'He's made a lovely job of my hair' [Integrated Adult/Child]

> M: 'He sure has - your hair looks gorgeous! You must feel really pretty!' [Integrated Parent/Adult/Child]

Or, while your head is buried in the fridge:

> M: 'Hi honey. Been to the hairdressers? How do you feel?'

> F: 'Terrible! He's made a real mess! He's cut it wrong over my ears and the color is awful!' [Integrated Adult/Child]

Only then can you turn to look at her and say:

> M: 'Yes I see what you mean - you must feel really upset!' [Integrated Adult/Child]

Avoid all attempts to find any solutions to her problem, unless she moves to Adult and asks plainly, clearly and specifically for your assistance.

Responding emotionally

You have to respond to her 'Emotional intelligence' by using emotional words and phrases. This means:

You **don't** ask what she *thinks* of something. [Adult]

You **don't** ask her *opinion* regarding something. [Adult]

Look at the words in *italics* in the list on the next page – they're emotive words - language that belongs to the emotional sphere.

Double meanings

But this not as simple as you would like. **Some of these words can be used in both an <u>emotional</u> *and* a <u>cognitive</u> way.**

Words like 'sense, 'suggest', 'impression' and 'instinct' can be used in an 'emotional' sense or a 'cognitive' sense. When you say to another male 'What *sense* do you make of this?' both of you will think in logical terms - about ideas, theories, concepts or solutions. 'What *cognitive* sense do they make of this?' But when your girlfriend says, 'What sense do you make of this', she may well be operating in her emotional sphere, asking, 'What do you *feel* about this?'.

Instead, you ask:

What do you *feel* about this?

How does this '*grab*' you?

Does this *resonate* with you at all?

What *impression* do you have about this?

What is your *sense* of this?

What *vibes* does this give you?

Do you have a *hunch* about this?

Does this *suggest* anything?

Do you have an *instinct* about this?

What is your *intuition* concerning this?

You *have a nose* for this - what do you *feel*?

Do you have any *inkling* about this?

Do you *fancy* this?

Is this *pleasing*?

Which of these would you *desire*?

Do any of these *excite* you?

Which of these would make you *happiest*?

Do either of these *thrill* you?

Are you *inclined* to any of these?

When she *seems* to be using *cognitive* words and phrases, it's very easy for you to slip into your natural, default cognitive mode - into your Adult. But it's best to remember that *she* is almost certainly operating in her *emotional* sphere, which means that the cognitive-sounding words and phrases that she uses actually have an *emotional* meaning.

> # Recognize that most of her statements are emotionally, not cognitively based

When you recognise that she talks in emotional terms, you can avoid many difficulties. For her, *it does not matter what the facts are* – what she is saying is that this is *undoubtedly what she feels at this present moment.*

When you recognize that these are emotive and not cognitive statements, you are freed up with regards to your responses.

So we have already seen -

You don't have to find solutions

She's not asking for solutions (Cognitive) but for emotional support and empathy. You are freed from the burden of solving her problems. In fact you hardly have to give her problem any thought whatsoever. There is a sense in which the *particular* problem that she presents to you - terrible world; awful boss - *is totally irrelevant.* **The issue is *how she is feeling in the present moment.*** She wants your agreement to confirm her emotional state, so she can feel a sense of belonging, security and empathy with you. Because she's not presenting you with a *cognitive* statement, you don't have to think up any counter-arguments or think up any clever answers or solutions.

When it comes to how she feels –

> *You can always agree with her*
>
> *statements about how she feels*

So, here is the tactic:

> Turn her seemingly cognitive
>
> statement into a statement about
>
> how she feels right now -
>
> *and agree with it*

You can agree with whatever emotive statement she makes. She's telling you how she *feels,* and you have no reason to doubt it. Your first word of reply has to be **'Yes!'**

When you agree with her, she hears that you have heard how she feels.

Male and female listening

Females often say that males don't listen, but females don't always listen either. But the *way* in which they don't listen is different: males are absorbed in their own projects and tasks, so they only half-listen; but females also use selective hearing. When you make a statement that strongly resonates with her present emotional undercurrent, she stops listening. This emotion now completely dominates her thoughts – 'emotional intelligence' - and sends her down detours.

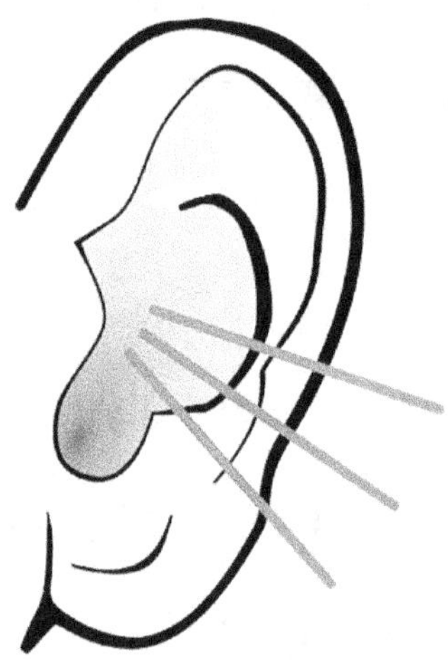

But you can use her selective listening to your advantage. When you say - 'Yes!' - in response to her emotional statement, this will probably be all that she will hear and want to hear. When she hears you say 'Yes', or 'That's true!' or 'I agree', she will instantly feel that she's no longer alone, isolated, excluded or insecure - your agreement will give her the sense of inclusion, belonging, connection and security with you that she needs.

When you agree, *you are **not** saying that you agree with the logic or cognitive position that she has expressed.* You are **not** agreeing that the world is terrible, or that her boss is a bastard, or that the neighbors are nosey. But you can still agree with her because you are agreeing that

this is what she feels, and that

you have heard that this is what she feels right now.

All you have to do is to 'mirror' or reflect back what she says. You do this by *repeating her statement back to her as **a reflection of her feelings***.

So you add and repeat her statement to your agreement:

M: 'Yes, I can see that you **feel** that the world is a terrible place.'

Or:

M: 'True, I can see that you **sense** that those people across the road are nosey.'

Or:

M: 'I agree that you **fancy** that there are too many immigrants in this country.'

At the very worst, you can say -

M: 'Yes, I can see that's how you **feel**.'

Once you master this skill, she will feel that you are listening and sympathetic - **and** you also succeed in putting the responsibility for her 'felt opinion' back where it belongs – it's *her* feeling/opinion reflected back to her *as **her** feeling/opinion* and you are agreeing with how **she** feels *rather than agreeing with the opinion itself.*

Unfortunately a single agreement like this will not end the

matter. She wants reassurance and it will probably not be achieved by one simple agreement from you.

She'll continue to make similar statements **until her feelings of insecurity / uncertainty / aloneness subside**. Your aim is to give her maximum reassurance, minimizing the time you spend on this (to you) load of nonsense.

An exception to the 'not finding a solution' principle

I've said that 'You don't have to find solutions.' But I'm not saying that you *never* have to find solutions. There are times when she genuinely wants you to help her to find a solution to her problem.

So how do you know when she genuinely wants you to help her find a solution to a problem? The clue is in her position. If she's in Child, she almost certainly has an emotional base to her statements and requires your agreement. You respond in Parent and come alongside her like a listening Parent, your role being to agree with her to confirm how she feels and to reassure her that it's O.K..

However, if she's in Adult, she's at her *least* emotional and *most* cognitive. She may genuinely be seeking a solution to a problem and be asking you to help her by bringing your cognitive skills to the matter. If she's in Adult but you respond by agreeing with her emotional state, it will seem to her that you are being dismissive, patronizing and not taking the issue seriously.

> When she's in Adult, you may well have to try to find solutions

Another word of warning

Hopefully you are starting to understand how and why females act and speak the way that they do. But females like to think that they have some sort of mystique and hidden intuitiveness - so it's best that you *never* tell her that you know what she thinks even if you think that you know *exactly* what she is thinking and feeling. When you 'see through' her ploys and tactics and tell her what she is thinking or feeling, she will feel vulnerable – she will feel that she has lost her air of mystery and even 'superiority'.

So:

> Never tell her that you know what she is thinking, even if you do know *exactly* what she is thinking and feeling

Back to males and females listening

Many females complain that males don't listen to them, but worse than this, some females complain that when males want to talk they expect females to give them their full attention and listen to him carefully.

When questioned further, the females who said that 'males don't listen' altered what they said to something like 'males only half listen', or 'what I say just doesn't go in', or 'they seem to hear but don't remember - even when prompted'. As one female put it: 'They are on man-planet'. As a male, you tend to focus narrowly or intensely and you tend to focus on the future. A typical female [Critical Parent] term for this is 'Tunnel Vision'.

If your girlfriend uses 'put downs' like 'Tunnel Vision', or 'He's on Man Planet', ignore the 'put down' and point out the advantages of your position:

> M: 'The great thing about tunnel vision is that there are no sidetracks. Get side tracked and you go into a brick wall. All I have to do is focus on the light at the end of the tunnel!'

Or:

> 'Having had tunnel vision all morning means that I've finished my work and so I can go home an hour early!'

As we have seen earlier, females have a broader, more diffuse focus in the here and now and so they claim to engage in so-called 'multi-tasking' - a seemingly noble term that really means 'Jill of all trades but mistress of none'. It's a fact that females talk more than males. Some of them give ongoing commentaries on what they or others are doing. They are also more focused on relationships and the home than males.

All of this means that when your girlfriend talks to you, it is indeed often true that you only half listen. This is because:

> Her conversation is probably interrupting a task or problem that is occupying your mind

> You may be very focused on what you are doing, so her conversation is a distraction - a hindrance disrupting your flow of thought

> Over time you have probably learned to place her constant chatter into the category of 'background noise', so that you pick up enough of it to agree or disagree in the right places. But in the main, her chatter is not worth your full, single-minded attention.

> She talks about subjects that don't engage your mind. Just as steam locomotives don't engage her mind, her themes of conversation don't engage your mind.

Hence the comment by one male:

> M: 'Females talk too much, mainly about unimportant things'.

You are aware, I'm sure, of the female who doesn't engage in conversation when she is watching soap operas on television. If you try to talk to her you will get curt, dismissive, irritated responses.

As a male, you are in this sort of mode much more often than she is. If your girlfriend is like this when she watches soaps, then, when you are both in Adult, this is one way to show her 'where you are' most of the time - in the same sort of single minded, intense focus that she is in when she watches soaps.

If she refuses to recognize this and continues to insist on talking to you and distracting you when your mind is focused on a problem, project or work, then tell her:

> M: 'Since you insist on talking to me and distracting me from what I'm doing instead of waiting until I can give you my full attention, I'll talk to you when you next try and watch your favorite soap'. [Disciplinary Parent threatening deterrent]

If you make this threat, *then carry it through*. When she gets annoyed, you point out that now she knows how *you feel* when she talks to *you* when *you* are busy [Emotive connection].

She may tell you that the two situations are 'completely different' [Parent. Emotional intelligence]. If she says something like this, get her to explain to *your* satisfaction *how* and in *what way* they are different [Male Parent drawing out Female Adult]. She probably won't be able to answer, and insist that 'They are just different. *Any fool* can see that they are different' [Parent Emotional intelligence]. Even so, keep insisting that she explains to you how they are so different, since it is so obvious to her but not to you, a mere fool.

Be prepared for her to get irritated, angry and start swearing and insulting you [Child]. If she swears, point out that she is close to the last refuge of someone who has lost the argument [Parent]. If she insults you stay in Parent and show that you are disappointed in her by 'tut-tutting' and shaking your head, or you announce that you are leaving if that is how she is going to speak to you or treat you [Parent, Withdrawal Deterrent].

The problem may be that it never *is* the right time for you to sit down and talk – you are wrapped up in your studies, absorbed in your own thoughts, or are more Childish and just want to focus on playing on the games console all the time. This failure on your part will draw out her Parent - Nurturing at first and then Critical.

So somehow, when you are both in Adult, you have to find a workable compromise. She has to understand that you are more narrowly focused and that random attempts to discuss something like domestic issues, as they occur to her in the present moment, are interruptions and that what she has to say may only be half listened to and may cause you to be irritated by the disruption. But you have to realize the down side of how you operate. You need to remember that she does like to have your full attention every now and again – it's a reasonable request - just like *you* like to have *her* full attention when *you* have something to say.

So:

Learn to take time to fully listen to her

Dealing with her 'present-moment' focus

Shopping

When you are both out shopping together, you will be focused on the goal but she will be diffusely focused in the present moment - differences that are deep rooted. Try to agree to spend a little time shopping separately, giving each other some individual shopping time.

'Multi-tasking'

I have suggested that 'multi-tasking' is a confidence trick invented by females who can only focus in a broad way in the here-and-now. If your girlfriend regularly says that she's able to 'multi-task' or that males – including you - are inferior because they can't 'multi-task', challenge the whole concept of 'multi-tasking' confidently and loudly:

F: 'Typical man - he can only do one thing at a time! Not like us women who can 'multi-task'. [Critical parent]

M: 'Multi-tasking is a myth!' [Parent. Dismissive tone]

F: 'It is not!'

M: 'Of course it is! It's confidence trick invented by you females who can't focus enough!' [Critical Parent.

Dismissive tone with condescending humor]

F: 'Women *can* do more than one thing at a time.'

M: 'They can! [Fogging] They just can't do any of them very effectively – they're a 'Jill of all trades and mistress of none!' [Parent. Wry smile]

F: '*You* can't multi-task – you're a man.' [Critical Parent]

M: 'Of course I can't multi-task [Fogging] - it doesn't exist - I do one job at a time and do it properly!' [Parent Disbelief and humor at the very idea of multi-tasking]

Once you've laid down this challenge you can focus on the female who uses the 'multi-tasking' fallacy the most, and *every time* she makes a mistake or fails to do something, you point it out. For example, she drops some office papers on the floor:

M: 'Oh! Is that a multi-task failure? Did you try to do more than one thing at a time and fail?' [Parent with a wry smile].

You use the **'Is that a multi-task failure?'** comment every time she fails, makes a mistake, has an accident, drops something and so on. You use it *relentlessly and without fail* until she learns to stop 'boasting' about her ability to multi-task.

'Multi-tasking' is a myth

Always challenge females who

insist it's a fact

Her need to belong

You may thrive on independence and individuality but females are often unsettled by being individual and independent because they sense that they are marginalized and isolated. So you may come across this kind of conversation -

M: 'I was talking about you to my mate today.' [Adult]

F: 'Oh? What about?' [Adult or Insecure Child]

M: 'I said that you have a mind of your own. You don't just do what I ask.' [Adult]

F: 'Oh! And what else did you say about me?' [Indignant, Insecure Child]

If you tell your girlfriend you have been talking about her with your mate, you may immediately engage her need to belong as well as her sense of isolation – she is being talked about behind her back. The fact that you have talked about her *and she wasn't there* and therefore doesn't know what you've said, makes her feel isolated and marginalized, which in turn makes her feel insecure, hence her indignant questioning.

> In general conversation, never create feelings of isolation, aloneness or exclusion in her unless you are in open warfare

It is when she is in Child that her need to belong is at its strongest. When she isn't getting her own way, or getting the attention she craves, she may act as a 'party pooper'. She may decide at the last moment that she isn't going to the party / meal with you, and if she doesn't go out with you then her 'emotional intelligence' informs her that you will *feel* the need to belong as well, and so you will stay with her and not go out either. (Have you still got that length of string so that you can find your way back out of the labyrinth again?).

Even though you are more independent than this, her tactic may put you in conflict. This is an example of **the 'cleft-stick' trap**. She puts you into a position whereby you are 'damned if I do, damned if I don't'. If you go out - you are being disloyal, if you stay in - you are one down, missing out and possibly letting your friends down.

In these kinds of scenarios, do what *you* want to do and certainly don't allow your plans to be changed by her whims:

> M: 'O.K. You stay in if you want to. I'm going to the party / meal anyway because I'm looking forward to it.' [Parent]

She may now feel excluded from both you *and* the group at the party / meal, and she may either:

Change her mind and come out with you after all, or

Become angry that you're going out anyway and still not giving her the attention she craves. She may well try another emotional tactic to try to drag you into the emotional swamp, such as 'Don't you love me any more?'

The cleft stick trap

Girlfriends often use the '**cleft stick trap**' to make you feel that you are 'damned if I do, damned if I don't', or to cut off and block your alternative solutions to a problem.

Here's an example:

F: 'The newspaper hasn't been delivered again. You'll have to do something about it.' [Parent]

M: 'I'll telephone the newsagent.' [Adult or Obedient

Child]

F: 'No don't telephone them, I'll feel awkward when I have to go into the shop.' [Adult/Child]

M: 'Perhaps we should cancel the delivery and I'll pick a paper up myself after work.' [Adult]

F: 'Don't be silly! You don't have time to do that!' [Parent]

M: 'Well we either tell the newsagent or we cancel the delivery and get the paper ourselves.' [Adult]

F: 'No. I don't want to phone them and we can't cancel the delivery. You'll have to do *something*.' [Parent. Cleft stick trap]

In these situations you can do one of two things: You can:

Do what you want anyway and clearly say so, or

Hand the problem over to her since your solutions seem to be unacceptable.

Thus:

F: 'No. I don't want to phone them and we can't cancel the delivery. You'll have to do *something*.' [Parent Cleft stick trap]

M: 'Well since you don't like my solutions [Adult] I'll leave it to *you* to sort it out to *your* satisfaction.' [Male Parent Withdrawal Deterrent]

You can bet your bottom dollar that this response will result in a critical response from her.....

F: 'Call yourself a man?' [Critical Parent]

Or:

> F: 'Can't you make a decision?' [Critical Parent]

These are diversionary tactics – detours. Keep focused on the problem at hand:

> M: 'Yes, I do call myself a man and since you don't like my manly solutions I'll leave it to you to sort it out to your feminine satisfaction.' [Critical Parent restating Withdrawal Deterrent]

Or:

> M: 'Yes, I *can* make a decision and my decision is that since you don't like my solutions I'll leave it to you to sort it out to *your* satisfaction.' [Critical Parent restating Withdrawal Deterrent]

The Lemming-group trap

Groups of females tend to be dismissive of males, and you are probably only too happy to get away from such groups by going to the bar, games console or train set. But sometimes it's less easy to walk away.

For example, your girlfriend invites you to her office Christmas party. You arrive to find that all her co-workers are female. At first, this may seem like heaven to you, but you are now caught in a brood of females - all of them talking about female subjects. Worse still, the entire brood, Mother Hen and Queen Bee included, are in Child or Parent position and this means that males tend to be excluded and/or criticised.

You have a couple of options.

After a short while, when you're bored of the crap chat about babies, illnesses and the price of washing powder, you say -

> M: 'Let's stop talking crap now.' and say this with a big charming smile to avoid any hostility. [Integrated Parent/Child]

In your Parent, you take charge of the theme of the conversation, allowing your Child to give an element of charm, humor and mischief. You have to have good conversational skills, being able to start new themes and keep the conversation going. You *may* succeed in getting the chat around to more interesting themes.

Remember! This is exactly what a girlfriend in Parent does when she comes home to find you and your male friends in conversation. She gains control by stopping the flow of your conversation by changing the theme to one in which she can be included. *If it's good enough for her - it's good enough for you.*

Stop the flow of conversation by cutting

across the female chatter to change

the theme of the conversation

Another option is that you can start *blatantly flirting* with one or some of the other females [Integrated Parent/Child]. This activity is almost certain to get your girlfriend's full attention. She may well feel excluded from the new group you have created [A Parental ploy exploiting her need to belong]. She may also feel jealous [Child] that other females are engaged in flirty conversation with you whilst she is excluded [A Parental ploy putting her into Child and exploiting her Child vulnerabilities]. This approach may also break up at least some of the girly-girl group. Of course she may become angry with you for daring to talk to other females [Child]. Ensure that you have already defined the Boundary Line that states that you will talk to other females whether she is with you or not. Remind her of this or say:

M: 'Since you weren't interested in talking to me I decided to find some women who *were* interested in me.' [Authoritarian, Parent with less Child humor. Withdrawal Deterrent by removing your presence from her].

Divide and conquer by giving

other females a lot

of charming attention

'Tit-for-tat' tactics

Your girlfriend's 'present moment need to belong' can make her seem clingy and make you feel claustrophobic because you are a more independently-minded male. For example, she's absorbed in soap operas - but insists that you stay in the room with her even though she gives you no attention at all as she watches the soap. But you can't use a tit-for-tat tactic and insist that later on she stays in the same room with you while you watch 'Avengers assemble!'. It doesn't work.

Tit-for-tat tactics don't always work

because males and females

are different

She has an emotional need for you to 'be there' while she watches her soaps, but you don't need her to be there while you watch 'The Godfather'.

If she's watching soaps, you have a right to do something else. You may choose to go out but she doesn't trust you when you go out. This kind of thing is best dealt with when you are both in Adult; otherwise she will keep presenting you with non-rational emotional arguments to support her viewpoint. In Adult position you can both discuss the matter unemotionally and agree to set up boundary rules. Even so, when her emotions get hold of her again, she may want to override the rules you have both previously agreed.

Female insecurity, relationships and not listening

Insecurity is a core negative emotion for some girlfriends, an emotion that is often deeply rooted in her early childhood experience. As we have seen, girlfriends often complain that their boyfriends don't listen, but girlfriends don't listen either – especially insecure girlfriends. You may praise her independence to your mates when she's not there - but when she finds out that you were talking about her, she completely fails to hear the praise and moves the conversation so that you have to defend the fact that you were talking about her in her absence.

Here's another example:

You come home from work and tell your girlfriend about your day at work:

M: 'I've been very busy today, but I had a laugh with Sue who works next to me. [Girlfriend stops listening]. This guy came in wearing shorts - in the middle of winter! We laughed at how stupid he looked and could not stop laughing at one point.'

F: 'You get on with Sue do you?' [Child insecurity]

M: 'Yea. She's OK. We have a laugh sometimes.' [Adult]

F: 'Is she attractive?' [Child insecurity]

M: 'What?' [Adult]

F: 'She seems to like you. You obviously have lots of laughs together.' [Child insecurity]

M: 'We only laughed at this guy, that's all.' [Adult]

F: 'Do you fancy her?' [Child insecurity]

Your girlfriend stopped listening after you said 'I had a laugh with Sue'. Her insecurity was triggered by the fact that you seem to find a female work colleague attractive and obviously have a laugh with her. Her feelings of insecurity now *completely dominate* the conversation, sending it down a detour. Instead of sharing an innocent humorous incident, you now find that you are defending yourself against an indignant, interrogating girlfriend.

When your girlfriend goes down seemingly irrelevant or irrational detours, it gives away the fact that she is no longer listening. She changes the direction and tone of the conversation in a way that seems irrational and/or trivial to you – especially if you are in Adult. It may seem trivial at first, but the tone of her voice won't be. She may become angry, indignant or confrontational and she will stay with this new theme like a dog with a bone. She won't let it go. And you may be completely wrong-footed and become angry yourself:

M: 'Fu***** hell! All I was doing was sharing a bit of fun I had today! Now you're accusing me of being attracted to the female I work next to!' [Angry Child]

The direction that the detour takes gives an indication of her emotional insecurities, anxieties, fears, worries and concerns. In this example she is insecure about her ability to keep you and about her own attractiveness. Any hint that you enjoy the company of other females will trigger her insecurities such that she will no longer hear anything that you say. Any small incident that seems to confirm her insecurity will get her in touch with her deep-seated emotions, which will be out of proportion to the incident itself. She will project the cause of her unbearable emotions outwards – by disowning responsibility for them and putting the blame onto you – how she feels is *your* fault. In fact you were merely laughing with your female work colleague but as far as your insecure girlfriend is concerned, this may well be the start of a sexual affair that confirms that she is going to lose you because of her own unattractiveness. She may even feel that such an affair has been secretly going on for some time – she has suspected so all along. Her feelings are so intolerable that it *must* be your fault because you are an untrustworthy, unfaithful alpha male who is always looking opportunistically at other females.

These kinds of female insecurities are very difficult for you to counter. Your Adult reasoning and rationality does not work because she is functioning in her emotional sphere. Trying to reason with her by saying, 'I was only having a laugh with Sue', or, 'I only work next to Sue, that's all', or, 'I'm not attracted to her - we were just laughing at something' will probably not succeed. While she intensely feels her insecurities, she will counter all your rational arguments that contradict how she feels in the present moment. Only as her feelings of insecurity subside will she begin to stop acting like a dog with a bone and ease off with her accusations. It may seem to you that she changes because you successfully offer rational arguments, but your reasoning may have nothing to do with her calming down.

Since she is primarily in Child, the rational reasoning of your Adult is not really the position for you to adopt. If she persists in her detour, you may become frustrated and infuriated at your inability to rationally talk this matter through with her, and you begin to move to your emotional Child. But if you are dragged into your Child with her, then you will not only become emotional and angry, but possibly violent and threatening, or become upset and start crying or feel overwhelmed.

This leaves you with Parent - or does it? The problem here is not the fact that you were having a laugh with Sue at work. This is completely innocent. The problem is not the 'surface' presentation - laughing with Sue, or talking about your girlfriend with your mates. These are 'surface triggers' that get her in touch with her 'deeper' emotional concerns – such as childhood insecurity. This means that if you only deal with and talk about the presenting 'surface' issues, you will end up just tinkering about and 'scratching the surface' of a deep-rooted problem.

In Adult you can begin to 'uncover' and identify what these childhood insecurity issues are – you can more accurately identify her (or your) insecurities, where they originated from and what present day situations trigger them. If the problems caused by such insecurities are severe enough, it may mean turning to professional counseling.

You can of course move to Parent to deal with these issues:

F: 'Is she attractive?'

M: 'What?' [Adult]

F: 'She seems to like you. You obviously have lots of laughs together.'

M: 'We only laughed at this guy, that's all.' [Adult]

F: 'Do you fancy her?'

M: 'I think it's about time you grew up! Don't start accusing me because of your own insecurities! I'm off to the bar - the company is more pleasant there!' [Disciplinary Parent using Withdrawal Deterrent]

However, in moving to Parent you still only scratch the surface - you don't address the underlying problem. You may or may not move her out of Child into Adult, but her deeper sense of insecurity has not been addressed at all - instead it has been *repressed* – pressed down again - or 'put in a box' for now - but it will only burst out again later in response to another trigger.

Your girlfriend's insecurities can be quite specific, such as insecurity about her attractiveness, but some girlfriend's insecurities may be quite pervasive and general - fears and concerns about the world in general and about how she fits into the scheme of things.

To compensate for her general sense of anxiety, she may create quite a very definite, rigid view of the world, based on how she feels she would like the world to be. This 'rigid certainty' gives her a sense of order and a feeling of 'security'. But no one else understands her very particular and individual 'emotional conceptualisation' of the world very well at all, since it is based on her personal emotions. Worse still, her 'emotionally conceptualised model' of what the world is like often fails in its predictions:

> F: 'He said he was going to call this afternoon. Do you know what time he came to visit? Five o'clock. Five o'clock! What sort of time is that? I ask you! I'd been sitting there since three o'clock like a fool.'

Or:

> F: 'Her daughters are cooking Sunday lunch for her. They haven't even peeled a potato and it's two o'clock! I've never heard of such a thing! It's terrible! Wicked! Two o'clock and they haven't even started to prepare it. We always had Sunday lunch at one o'clock.'

Her insecurities are firmly based in her childhood experience, so when current events trigger these insecurities, she tends to move to Child such that her personal emotional insecurities from childhood dominate her thoughts and behavior and **prevent her from listening**, as well as setting her off on her detours.

Her emotional concerns may be to do with her sense of belonging:

> How she should be in the world

> About relationships or social groups in general

> About 'What folks will think',

> 'Keeping up appearances' and

> About how things or people look

So you might hear things like this:

> F: 'Look at those two laughing over there! He looks like a midget compared to her. Do you think that they're married?'

Her emotional insecurities may be about her status in relation to other females in the girly-group that she belongs to - will she move up in the pecking order, or move down. She may want to obtain information 'on the sly', information that she feels will give her 'status' and a feeling of security in the group, or information that she can use to gain alliances that will make her feel more secure. By brooding together with like-minded females she may obtain a sense of 'security' - there is safety in numbers.

Here are some examples:

M: 'I saw cousin James in the bar the other day.' [Adult]

F: 'Was his son with him?'

M: 'I don't know.'

F: 'Does he still live at ......?'

M: 'I have no idea.'

F: 'Does he still live with that Blonde?'

M: 'I just said 'hello' that's all.'

Or:

M: 'I called at Dorothy's and got your theatre tickets.'

F: 'Was Josie there?'

M: 'No'

F: 'Had she been earlier?'

M: 'I don't know'

F: 'When had Josie last called?'

M: I haven't the foggiest idea.'

F: 'Did Dorothy say that Josie was going call?'

M: 'No.'

F: 'Josie wasn't there then?'

M: 'No.'

She stopped listening after 'I called at Dorothy's....' because she became concerned about Josie and whether there is any sort of alliance between Dorothy and Josie that she is excluded from or doesn't know about.

Or:

1st F: 'He gave Jill a beautiful gift. But you should have heard what he said to her.'

2nd F: 'What *did* he say?'

1st F: 'I can't say - but she wasn't very happy!'

2nd F: 'You must have *some* idea of what he said!'

1st F: 'Yes, but I can't repeat it.'

2nd F: 'You can tell me, I won't tell anyone.'

1st F: 'Well.....Don't say anything to Dorothy but it was something about her husband, but I can't say any more.'

This is a power play by the first female who has access to information that the second female wants to gain. The first female can act from a powerful position as a dispenser of knowledge, and she creates both curiosity and dependency in the second female.

Quite labyrinthine plots can develop in this way - 'Don't say anything to Dorothy but...' You get caught in these kinds of things at your peril. They cause family arguments, fall-outs at work, divisions between friends and so on. Don't be drawn into such schemes, rumors and gossip and state quite plainly:

M: 'This is female talk! I'm not interested! [Parent]

Female Parent and the 'empty nest' syndrome

Some females behave towards their male partners as if are substitute children who need mothering. Even younger girlfriends may do this. 'Mother' is an aspect of Parent and such girlfriends tend to place you in your Child as if you are a hopeless, helpless naughty little boy who can't think for yourself. She will complain that you are 'always under her feet', and speak to you (or at you) as though you are an inferior species, using harsh comments and cutting remarks.

F: 'Does your sense of humor improve when you've had a drink? Let's hope so.' [Critical Parent]

You allow her to continue like this at your peril - she will organize you, tell you how to dress, what to eat, when to eat it and how to eat it, and will become a nag.

You resist fully entering your Child position because this would make you weak and you would be putting yourself two down.

You could try 'running with the ball' that she has thrown:

> F: 'Does your sense of humor improve when you have had a drink? Let's hope so.' [Critical Parent]

You top up her glass from the bottle of wine on the table, full to the brim, so it is difficult for her to pick up without spilling the contents and say:

> M: 'Let's hope a good drink makes *you* more attractive, but I doubt it' [Critical Parent]

Then, open your wallet, pay for the meal that you (**and only you**) have had, and leave [Withdrawal Deterrent].

A girlfriend in her Parent position will resist your attempts to move to your Adult or Parent, still seeing you as a naughty defiant little boy, so she tries to maintain the crossed relationship.

Recognise this pattern and challenge it. Refuse to let her place you in Child and move to Parent, (unless she moves to Adult). Challenge her openly and have your withdrawal strategies ready to use.

You could be very blunt:

> M: 'Who do you think you're talking to? Don't speak me in that tone of voice.' [Indignant Parent] Then leave the room. [Withdrawal deterrent]

Or you could soften your approach using humor:

> M: 'I wasn't aware you'd become my mother! When

did that happen?' [Parent using Child humor]

She will almost certainly challenge you, out of habit if nothing else, and so she will still treat you like a naughty child who is challenging her Parental 'authority'. She may well *increase* her Parental efforts to keep you in line and make you do as you are told:

> F: 'You *need* a mother because you are so *useless*!' [Critical Parent]

In this kind of situation you have to move to authoritarian, disciplinarian, humorless Parent - a rival 'authority' to her Mother/Parent. In the process you may create potential confrontation:

> M: 'We'll see how useless I am when you want some money for shopping!' [Parent, Withdrawal Deterrent]

Often, such females are blind to what they doing. They don't see themselves as a 'superior authority', but as supporting and helping you by keeping house and home 'together'.

If you can catch her in Adult, you move to Adult as well and talk to her openly and plainly about how she tends to demean you and how you don't like it. Together, you may be able to set up new boundary rules, but be prepared, because underneath all her 'mothering', she may feel vulnerable, and have a sense of purposelessness and these feelings may well flood to the surface if the mask of her 'superiority' has been taken away.

Always challenge her 'Parent' by refusing to let her place you in Child. Be prepared for her to increase her Parental tactics and/or for her to get in touch with an emotional identity crisis

The 'empty nest' is the family home. A nurturing Parental female has placed a lot of focus, time and energy on the home - something you don't share to the same degree. Many of her complaints about you will center on the home:

Not putting clothes away

Leaving coat hangers on doors

Dumping wet towels on the bed

Not putting milk back in the fridge

Not cleaning the bath after using it

Not putting the toilet seat down

The worst is missing your aim when you go to the toilet.

Company Motto: We aim to please – will you aim too please

Your eating habits will be criticised - talking with your mouth full, rushing your food, slurping your drink and so on. She will accuse you of being lazy around the house - you don't know how the washing machine works for example. When she asks you to do a job around the house, you are criticised for doing it grudgingly, or for cutting corners.

Sometimes she's right - she tidies the house and then through your carelessness you undo all her hard work. Most of us males need to be more thoughtful around the home and take a bit of effort to keep things tidy.

But,

When she asks you to do a job and then keeps complaining that you're not doing it quickly enough, or to the right standard, then you're best telling her to do the job herself. She knows what speed and standard she wants so she's best seeing to the task herself. [Male Parent]

If you can't do a household chore to her satisfaction, make her to do it herself

Us males put different aspects of our lives - work, home, leisure and so on, into separate 'boxes' in our mind. For you, if your home is reasonably clean, tidy, comfortable and warm, then you are happy - your home will not figure very large in your awareness. You may regard domestic chores as 'woman's work' - *she* is the one who always fusses about the home. So you may find that you put household chores into a box labelled 'women's work'. Your mind is then free to consider other matters.

Blind spots and domestic chores

Both you and your girlfriend have blind spots. For you, they tend to center on household chores. Your girlfriend may look on these as being *shared* responsibilities but you see them as *her* responsibility. [Lack of Boundary Rules]. You walk into the kitchen where there is a pile of dishes, but it does not register in your mind to wash them. You *see* them, but that's as far as it goes. Or she's put clothes in the washing machine that has now finished its cycle so the washing is ready to peg out - but you don't even see them. You half notice the layer of dust on the table but do nothing about it. Your solution? Play on the Playstation. This is because *you are not looking for these kinds of tasks* because **you have allocated them to her under 'woman's work'**. The wet washing is 'woman's work in progress' - 'woman's work half done' - who knows what the plan is for this washing. You think that it's not your place to intrude on someone else's work. When she picks you up on these things you may feel as though you are becoming a domestic slave.

The allocation of such domestic tasks may have been established legitimately when you were both in Adult as part of Boundary Rule setting. Even if these tasks have been clearly allocated to your girlfriend, she may still complain that you are not dealing with these chores - she changes the rules based on how she's feeling in the present moment. If you protest that these are *her* chores she'll complain that you are inflexible and that she has to do *everything*. ['Emotional intelligence']

If you live alone, such domestic tasks will be part of your routine – there's no one else to do them. If you don't wash the dishes or do the laundry no one else will. In this situation, these domestic tasks enter your awareness and you work out a routine to get them done. You may even become very particular with regards to being tidy around your house/apartment.

But your girlfriend will have blind spots too. She doesn't notice that the drain has been unblocked, shelves have been put up, the faulty light switch has been replaced, the garden has been maintained, fence painted, guttering cleaned, car maintained and so on. For many girlfriends these things seem to happen automatically.

So, let's come back to domestic chores. Break down the chores that you do into their component parts and mention each part to her so that you get 1 point for *each component* rather than 1 point for the whole task.

If she accuses you of not noticing household chores you have two options. You can:

> Insist that you both agreed that these are *her* responsibilities and that picking up such jobs when

> they are half completed is not your responsibility - you have your own allocated tasks.

Or,

> Take a softer approach and look to how aware you are of these things.

With this second option, make a checklist of items to tick off when you come home each day - a set of prompts to remind you of what might need doing - any dishes to wash, dry and put away, any washing to peg out, any cleaning or dusting that needs doing, any litter bins to empty. Once again, if you do any of these always mention them to her to get 1 point for each.

If she is critical of your efforts, immediately go into disciplinary Parent and say:

> M: 'I was only trying to help you out because you failed to do/complete your chores. Since you don't appreciate my help I won't bother in future.' [Withdrawal Deterrent]

In this way, Boundary Rules are re-established. Boundary Rules need to be detailed and very well defined when it comes to household chores, so that roles are clear. It's no use saying something like 'Whoever sees that the litter bin is full should empty it.' This rule is far too vague. It will always be *your* fault if the bin is not emptied. Far better to allocate specific chores to a specific person so that responsibility is clear and well defined.

You can also agree that if she does something like putting laundry in the washing machine and setting the machine running before she goes out, then if she wants *you* to peg out the washing when you come home, *she must leave a note* for you, or she must phone or text you, plainly asking you to peg the washing out [Boundary Rule]. You get her to clearly state what she wants – she must never rely on the off chance that you may notice the clothes in the machine and take this as a hint that they should therefore be pegged out.

Take care!

She may take advantage of this rule by regularly leaving a whole list of tasks that the you should, ought or must do [Parent]. In this way she starts to control your free time at home and then she becomes critical of you if these tasks are not done. In this case you have to reset the Boundary Rule - such notes, phone messages or texts are not an agenda of tasks that she thinks up for you to do so that she doesn't have to do them, such notes are only there to draw your attention to her request for you *to finish off something that she started but was unable to finish* – something that you otherwise might not notice.

In response to the idea of leaving you notes she may protest that she shouldn't have to write notes. You tell her that she *does* have to write notes if she wants her unfinished chores attending to. No note – no guarantee that you will finish her chores for her.

Clearly define who does what

household chores and

when they do them

The do it yourself handyman

It may be that you are the kind of guy who spends a great deal of time carrying out do-it-yourself work. Some males always seem to be doing some job or other around the house - and they do so for different reasons than females. She is a 'nest builder', but males get involved in 'projects', the completion of which gives them a sense of achievement and satisfaction.

But some males have different projects, which take the form of a hobby such as building a working model railway or a operating a radio-controlled model. For some it may mean a mechanical engineering project such as building a working steam engine, or tinkering with the car in the garage - taking the wheels off, putting them back again and so on. For yet others, gardening may be their project - working in an allotment growing vegetables to sell, or working on the garden that belongs to the house. For some males, their 'project' is the house itself, getting involved in challenging jobs from plastering, to plumbing, to electrical work, to decorating, to carpentry. For the D-I-Y enthusiast, house projects are never fully completed – there's always something else to do.

A girlfriend partnered with a male who is a handy D.I.Y man can gain the advantage of her 'nest' looking up to date and modern - if she can tolerate the 'mess' that occurs when the jobs are being done that is.

Many girlfriends think that *all* males are D.I.Y experts and handymen who are competent at carrying out jobs around the home including:

Removing a big spider from the bath

Plastering a wall

Putting up shelves

Mending a broken washing machine

Mending a broken central heating boiler

Hanging wallpaper

Painting

Hanging a door

Repairing a garden fence

Fixing a dripping tap

Removing a wall radiator

Some males are indeed blessed with the ability, interest and set of skills that enable them to carry out these jobs competently. But equally, many males are *not* blessed with these skills and they have no inclination to learn them.

Some girlfriends equate such skills with *manhood* –

> F: 'You can't fix the dripping tap? And you call yourself a man?' [Critical Parent]

If you aren't a D.I.Y handyman, best to say so as soon as you sense that the relationship is getting serious. Put it bluntly and plainly:

> M: 'By the way, you should know that I'm no good at D.I.Y. jobs. If you want a handyman, I'm not that man - you need someone else.' [Parent]

Then, whenever she asks you to carry out any D.I.Y. jobs around the house that are beyond your skills, you can refuse to do them and remind her that you told her right at the start of the relationship that you were not a handyman.

> If you are not skilled at doing jobs
>
> around the house - state this fact
>
> very early on in the relationship

Using the female reward system

Save yourself a lot of worry and expense by remembering that she gives one point for *everything* and work this to your favor.

Look at this list:

Buy her:

A single rose	- 1 point
An expensive bouquet of flowers	- 1 point
A pub lunch	- 1 point
An expensive meal in a top restaurant	- 1 point
A coke	- 1 point
Champagne	- 1 point

Don't waste your money buying a huge bouquet of flowers every time - a medium bunch of flowers occasionally or single rose once a week is enough - all of these options score one point, so you can save a lot of money. Save the bouquet for Valentine's Day, an anniversary or her Birthday e.t.c..

Everything you do, every gift you buy, regardless of size or expense, is worth 1 point. Save your money - don't do expensive all the time

Break down the tasks you do into smaller components so that it looks like this:

What did you do?

I stripped the wallpaper on Monday - (1 point),

I repaired the wall on Tuesday - (1 point),

I put on the undercoat on Wednesday - (1 point),

I painted the gloss on Thursday - (1 point) and then

I wallpapered on Friday - (1 point),

    equaling a total of FIVE points.

Don't do the scoring for her - just tell her what you've done and break it down into its component parts so that you multiply your reward points even though you've done exactly the same amount of work.

Describe the whole task it's worth 1 point. Break it down into smaller tasks and *each part* is worth 1 point

Also remember that she scores every mistake that you make. *Never* let *her* misbehavior or mistakes go unmentioned. If *she's* point scoring then you can *both* start scoring.

> ## She keeps score of all your mistakes and failures - do the same with her

She won't like her misbehavior being pointed out to her. She will use diversionary tactics in the hope that her own mistakes will be bypassed or forgotten.

Point out her misbehavior with a disbelieving tone of voice -

> M: 'You are keeping tabs and spying on *me*?' [Authoritarian/Disciplinarian Parent]

Or:

> M: 'You are reading *my* text messages on *my* phone?' [Authoritarian/Disciplinarian Parent]

She will then use diversionary tactics –

> F: 'Yea, but no, but.....'

Or:

> F: 'Bovvered?' [Child]

She will then divert right back to restate *your* mistake or failure. Dismiss such tactics and return to a sharp focus on *her* misbehavior, refusing to be diverted:

> M: '*You* may not be bothered but *I am* bothered that you're reading *my* text messages on *my* phone.' [Authoritarian/Disciplinarian Parent]

Or:

> M: 'I don't care about 'yes but'...*I* care that you're reading *my* text messages on *my* phone.' [Authoritarian/Disciplinarian Parent]

Unswervingly refuse to be diverted so that in every sentence you bring the conversation back to *her* misdemeanor

[Parent]. This way, she won't forget the times that *she* makes mistakes or misbehaves and she knows that *you* have not forgotten them either.

Paying her compliments

Your girlfriend is almost certainly a compliment junkie – especially in Child position - she can't get enough of you telling her how vibrant, slim, pretty, sexy e.t.c. she is. But the more you give her, the more she wants and whatever you give her earns just one point. So be careful with your compliments and praise - ***ration them.***

Paying her an unasked for compliment out of the blue – 'You look radiant this morning! What have you done?' - will nearly always earn you one reward point, providing

     a) You don't overdo it and/or

     b) You don't seem insincere

One compliment a week should be enough. Is it Tuesday? – it must be compliment day – providing she's been a good girl of course!

Talking too much and not talking enough

Females talk all the time. Whereas a male may *think* 'I'll tidy the living room and put the magazines away', your girlfriend may actually *say it out loud.*

This male quietness can be a disadvantage. You come home to find that your girlfriend has cut the lawn and it looks neat and tidy. You note how neat the garden looks and think to yourself that she has done a good job. Then you move on to your own tasks – you've got to clean your car, have a shower, sort out some financial matters and so on. When your girlfriend returns home, she gets no comments from you about the lawn. You've moved on to the next future-orientated goal. After a while she may say 'Have you noticed the garden?' and then you may indeed say that you had noticed it and that it looks very neat. Unfortunately, this is too late. It was not noticeable enough for you to make a comment so your comments *after* her prompt are at best faint praise. Zero points on the reward system. Zilch.

Make the effort to catch yourself when you are merely thinking that she's done something well, and then express your thoughts to her, before you become focused on the next goal. Text her or phone her to say 'The garden looks great!' That's all it takes. You've now appealed to her Child Vanity and compliment junkie. In effect you've said 'Good girl!' and she's pleased that you've noticed. One point!

Get into the habit of telling her every so often how much you value who she is and what she does - without having to be prompted by her

Chivalry - right or wrong?

There was a time when males on crowded buses or trains readily stood up for a female if all the seats were occupied. In the same way males opened doors for females and so on. This actions are a form of chivalry. Some females like (or even expect) this kind of behavior and may say that males who make such gestures are a 'gentleman'. (I'm not you know!). They may walk up to a door with their boyfriend and stop in front of it, expecting and waiting for him to open the door for her.

These days however, some females see such behavior as insulting. Perhaps it makes them feel like an invalid, or incapable, or puts them in touch with feeling old. Some may even feel that the male is making a sexual advance. So what should you do? Should you be chivalrous by habit or not?

Feminists and the so-called equality of the sexes have altered the balance. These days, many females like to think that they are independent, self-sufficient and equal with males or even superior to them.

If your girlfriend is offended by such a chivalrous gesture on your part, you have two options:

> Move to Parent and tell her face-to-face that you were looking after her, but that you won't look after any more. [Parent, Withdrawal Deterrent and Boundary Rule change]

Or,

> If you are genuinely offended by her critical attitude, say: 'And *I* am offended by *your* attitude towards me. If it happens again, this relationship is over.' [Male Parent. Threat of Withdrawal Deterrent].

In making this threat you are prepared to walk away if your threat is challenged.

But what if she expects such chivalrous behavior all the time, as if it is her right? Any *expectation* on her part to be given male chivalry as her right is part of her Child vanity. She may use her Child position in two ways.

> She may desire to be made a fuss of and love the feeling that being the center of attention gives her.

In this case move to Parent (because she is in Child) and indulge her whims with amusement and with mocking over-exaggeration of your chivalrous gestures. You bow too low as she goes through the door for example. But you give these gestures to her on your own terms for as long as it amuses you.

She may have strong *expectations* of chivalrous gestures all the time, as if she has an automatic right to be treated in this way. If so, she will become indignant, critical or despising of you when you show a lack of chivalry. She is still in Child but adopting a pretence to a Parental position. In effect, it is her Bossy Child.

In this case, move to Parent (because she is in Child), but this time to a more authoritarian or disciplinarian Parent, mellowed as always by your use of humor:

> M: 'I'll open the door when I see someone worthy enough to open the door for!' [Parent with Child humor]

Then you open the door for yourself and walk through it in front of her, leaving her standing there and having to follow on and open the door for herself.

When your girlfriend expects or demands chivalrous treatment, and she becomes critical at the lack of it, take her vanity down a peg or two.

So here is the first rule: you can volunteer chivalrous gestures - but she must not be allowed to expect or demand them from you. You only volunteer such gestures if she is being a 'good girl'.

You volunteer chivalrous gestures IF she is being a good girl – don't allow her to demand them as her right

In her 'Bossy Little Princess' Child, she'll start to demand what you should, must or ought to do in terms of opening doors for her, buying her drinks, buying her meals, giving up your seat and so on. If you put up with it for too long, you will be pigeonholed into your Obedient Child such that you end up constantly seeking to be her 'good little boy' looking after the needs of your 'superior' 'prize' Princess. Failure to be a 'good little boy' will often result in her displaying temper tantrums, being affronted, adopting a critical tone, a disappointed tone, withdrawing her affection, being a party pooper or any other number of Childish tactics to get you to do as you are told. You will be at least one down.

Your chivalrous actions place your girlfriend into a 'superior' or 'more worthy' position - one up - and put you into a lower position - one down. So you have to use gestures of chivalry carefully and wisely [Parent/Adult] to avoid the trap of your girlfriend always expecting you to be one down. When you are being chivalrous, you are volunteering to be one down *for a moment* - because it amuses you to adopt this position and to massage her Child vanity - to make her feel special and have your attention.

If your girlfriend is in her Adult position then you adopt your Adult position as well and treat her with respect, politeness and good manners. You may therefore choose to open doors for her, kiss her hand on first meeting or offer your help in any number of practical ways - which may include giving up your seat for her - all of these actions arising out of your sincere respect for her. In turn, she will understand that you are showing her respect and good manners.

How chivalrous you act towards females who are strangers is a totally different matter. She is a stranger and no conversation has taken place to help you discover what her position is, so it's difficult to work out what her reaction might be. A negative reaction produces withdrawal of your chivalrous gesture - for example, your seat is no longer offered to her and she has to remain standing. You can couple this with a statement such as:

> M: 'Forget it, I was only being polite and giving you the chance to sit down - I wasn't trying to get into your panties.' [Critical Parent]

Occasionally a female who you are not acquainted with may comment on the fact that you are *not* being chivalrous. For example, she may be sarcastic about you not holding a door open for her. In other words, even though she is a stranger, she still expects chivalrous treatment from you. But we have already seen that *females must not expect or demand chivalrous gestures from you.* **This principle is especially true when it comes to females who are not your friends or acquaintances.**

You can throw feminist type comments back to her when she says things like:

> F: 'Thanks for holding the door open.' [Critical Parent Sarcasm]

Or:

> F: 'Where have all the chivalrous gentlemen gone?' [Critical Parent Sarcasm]

Or:

> F: 'Don't you hold the door open for a lady?' [Critical Parent]

In any of these cases you can reply:

> M: 'Why? Are you disabled?'

Or:

> M: 'Why? Are you too old to open it yourself?'

Or:

M: 'When I *see* a lady I *will* hold the door open for her.'

All of these are said with a smile.

Females who express interest in you

Kerching!

At some point, you'll know that a female is expressing interest in you – she may tease you, test you or give you some sort of 'come on' – laughs, smiles, staring into your eyes and so on. As soon as you are aware of this *adopt a slightly detached attitude towards her.* This is even more important if she is pretty, attractive to males and knows it. She will be used to males fawning around her and offering her various 'sweeties' such as compliments, small gifts, wanting to dance with her and so on. By playing it cool and detached you go against what she's used to – her charms don't seem to work with you, so she has to try a little harder. She won't be sure whether she can't rest because she's attracted to you, or because she's angry with you for not being like the other 'young bucks' who give her lots of attention. Forget the 'sweets' and give her a taste of red hot pepper to aggravate her thirst.

As soon as you are aware that a female is interested in you, adopt a detached attitude towards her

You continue any relationship that develops by occasionally using this attitude of detachment so that she can't take you for granted. In this way you show her that you are not her 'obedient good little boy'.

Here's an example in the area of arranged 'phone calls – You know the situation – you've arranged to call her at a certain time – say nine o'clock tomorrow. If *you* have arranged to call her, make sure that you call her twenty to thirty minutes later than you arranged. By doing this you demonstrate that:

You set own agenda

She is not the most important female in the world to you (even if she is)

You are not her lapdog

In those twenty to thirty minutes you make her more aware of you and the relationship that she has with you – 'Did I do something wrong? Am I pretty enough? Who does he think he is?'

You put yourself one up.

'Ah!' you say, 'but what if *she* has arranged to call *me*?' Simple. Whatever time has been arranged, make sure you take her call – whether she calls on time or twenty minutes late. As soon as she calls, say something like:

'Hi! I'm just busy here, I'll ring you back in about ten minutes.'

Then, before she has time to say anything you hang up. *Twenty to thirty* minutes later, you ring her back. Have an excuse ready if she gets angry – you had to speak with your mother, help out your neighbor, attend to something important for work – whatever.

Never call when you say you will.

Never take the same approach twice in a row.

But next time you arrange to call, be punctual. This will stop you being boringly predictable, stop her from seeing you as being late all the time, and keep her wrong-footed and therefore interested.

8 FINAL THOUGHTS

Keeping your woman

This book is not about how to get a girlfriend and neither has it been about how to keep your girlfriend. Just the opposite, if you apply the approaches recommended in this book it means that you will be challenging the position that your girlfriend may have established and when you do so, she'll try to maintain or re-establish her dominant position. She may become even more Parental, put you down and criticize you even more, be more dismissive of you and will apply even more 'emotional intelligence' in trying to defend her own position. In short, the long-term effect of consistently using the approaches recommended in this book may actually lead to the failure of your relationship if she refuses to at least compromise or change to some degree. This collapse would be because of her failure to stay within the boundaries and roles that have been reasonably agreed between the pair of you or that have been requested by you.

Controlling your woman

Neither has this book been about you having dominance over your girlfriend, or about you controlling or manipulating her. It not a manual for always getting your own way, or for keeping her in an obedient and submissive relationship to you.

This is fantasyland O.K.? Such attempts at authoritarian control speak more about your insecurity, inadequacy or delusions than anything else. So this book is not about replacing the tyranny of the female with the tyranny of the male.

Self-control and self-determination

Rather, this book has been about your self-determination, self-governance and self-control within the context of a relationship with your girlfriend. It's been about gaining insight and understanding into why your girlfriend behaves the way that she does, and about recognizing the differences between male and female perceptions, needs and behaviors. It's been about recognizing how, why and when your girlfriend steps over the line in your relationship - about recognizing her attempts to control, manipulate and dominate your relationship - about how and why she breaks boundary rules. It's also been about suggesting some counter-approaches to these ploys in order to restore the correct balance. In short, it's been about giving you the insight, tools and approaches you need to stay in control of *yourself* rather than allowing your girlfriend to control you. It's been about giving you the insight, tools and approaches you need to stay true to yourself - to be true to who you are - instead of being shaped and even emasculated by your girlfriend into what her 'emotional intelligence' thinks/feels she wants you to be.

But if she can't accept you for who you are, if she can't accept the things that she doesn't like about you as well as the things that attract her to you, then she may well cause your relationship to fail, because she will either constantly nag you to change, or successfully get you to change and then say that you are no longer the man that she first met or even that you are no longer a man - period.

This book has been about you staying one up - about you not being prepared to compromise your manhood and who you are - about you determining your own life choices. Sure, you will compromise on some things - you will have to if your relationship is to be long-term and a success. Such compromises can be logically talked through and agreed upon by both of you getting together in your Adult orientations. If they can't be agreed upon, then your relationship is in trouble in that area. But the ultimate power that you have is your power to walk away - to simply refuse to compromise any further and to refuse to put up with her attempts to control and manipulate you.

Is a final solution possible?

So, is there a final solution? I said right at the outset that males and females are different. They are biologically and genetically different, therefore they are fundamentally and intrinsically different. We can't overcome these differences. When a male is brought up solely in a female environment - he ends up being emasculated. Female ideas about the 'new man' emasculate males and turn them into a domesticated servant. But in exactly the same way and for the same reasons, males can't get females to perceive, think, feel and behave as men do. Females who work in an exclusively male environment often lose some of their femininity - they begin to have tomboy characteristics and a rough and ready male humor, becoming in effect, 'one of the boys'. So trying to get a female to think, act and perceive like a male ends up being unsatisfactory as well. The fact that there are differences between males and females is not something that we have to merely accept and live with, it's something that we celebrate. It's these very differences that attract us to each other.

But these differences don't mean that your girlfriend must always have the upper hand, or that in some way she is 'superior' to you, even though females may often declare that this is the case. Nor does it mean that you must always give in to her alternative perspective out of some misguided sense of chivalry.

This book has been about you identifying and recognizing some of these differences and learning ways to respond to them in such a way that you keep your self-control and don't allow her to take over.

This means that very often, you have to adopt your Parent orientation, reigning in and confronting her 'superior' Parent, as well as the wayward elements of her Child orientation with withdrawal deterrents. But you encourage her acceptable Child qualities to stimulate her sense of romance, passion, energy, vitality, vibrancy and sexuality. You reign in the immature and weak elements of your own Child orientation, only allowing it to emerge to give you a controlled sense of mischief, humor, passion, energy and romance. You are on this ride for the duration of your relationship with a female.

Enjoy the thrill and spontaneity of the ride itself rather than being concerned about getting to the destination - whatever destination you think that may be. But remember: This book is for entertainment purposes only. The views expressed within it are those of the author alone and should not be taken as expert instruction or commands. The reader is responsible for his or her own actions. Neither the author nor the publisher assume any responsibility or liability whatsoever on behalf of the purchaser or reader of this material.

9 RESOURCES

The one thing that I can't do in a book is to provide examples or models of male behavior that you can watch and try to imitate. Fortunately however, there are movies out there that present you with some great examples of the themes we have looked at in this book.

In watching these films more closely, you can pick up on things that are difficult to portray in a book - like the character's tone of voice, their posture, their mannerisms such as smiles and winks and so on. The movies listed below feature not only strong males, but also strong female characters – both in Parent and in Child. You can watch and learn from great actors, actresses and writers, and play scenes a few times to really study the details of what is happening.

Many of the movies I have listed here are classic old movies because we are looking back to pre-feminist, pre-politically correct days when the qualities we are looking were more prominent. So you have to see beyond the back projection screens when characters are driving a car, past the studio-bound sets imposed by the then technical limitations, and get to the nitty-gritty of the stories, characters, dialogue and situations. Sometimes these titles have been remade in modern versions - but usually the originals are better, and these days, digital restoration means that these movies can be seen in the best quality possible.

To help you, I have made a few comments on each title but there are no story spoilers here, and all these movies have good reviews on IMDB unless otherwise stated.

Gone with the Wind (1939) Clark Gable, Vivienne Leigh. Gable plays the quintessential manly, devilish rogue, often epitomizing the male Parent orientation as Rhett Butler - romantically involved with fiery, feisty Scarlett O'Hara - often epitomizing the female Child orientation. The character of Melanie Wilkes provides the female Adult orientation whilst Ashley Wilkes is the male Child/Adult.

To catch a thief (1955) Cary Grant, Grace Kelly. Grace Kelly plays the perfect female Parent up against the ultra-cool, subtle and suave male Parent of Cary Grant - a crossed relationship that provides much of the background humor and the punch line of the film. Alfred Hitchcock directs.

Born to be Bad (1950) Robert Ryan, Zachary Scott, Joan Fontaine. Dir: Nicholas Ray. Robert Ryan - excellent as always - is an up and coming author and passionate rogue. Zachary Scott - also very good here - is a gentleman, passionless and rich. Joan Fontaine likes them both and wants them both. She wants the danger and passion that Ryan can give her - but at the same time she also wants the secure, luxurious millionaire lifestyle that Scott can offer her. How will these two 'real' men deal with her?

Angel Face (1952) Robert Mitchum, Jean Simmons. Young Jean Simmons takes a fancy to devilish rogue Bob Mitchum and she won't take no for an answer. Good ole Bob is the Bob that we would expect -

very manly, the master of 'I don't care' detachment expressing male Parent. Interesting to see a strong, willful female up against a strong, manly character. Worth analyzing just what it is that Bob does right and what he does wrong in this relationship.

Flamingo Road (1949) Joan Crawford, Zachary Scott, Sydney Greenstreet. Dir: Michael Curtiz. Zachary Scott plays the weak male to perfection here. He's a pawn of the corrupt town sheriff, played wonderfully by the excellent Greenstreet. (Devilish Male Parent). When Crawford (Female Adult) and Scott become romantically linked it threatens the sheriff's plans. So Crawford has to go....

Rampart (2011) Woody Harrelson - A superb character study of a devilish rogue that we get to know through the course of the film. Watch out especially for Harrelson picking up a female at a bar. Textbook stuff.

Home from the hill (1960) Robert Mitchum, Eleanor Parker, George Peppard, George Hamilton. Mitchum gives a perfect portrait of a man going beyond being a devilish rogue [Male Parent]. A film about sons growing up and turning from boys to men, and about the women they love. Mitchum's performance is mesmerizing in the light of the themes of this book - particularly watch out for how he uses facial expressions and his tone of voice when he *really* gets pissed off!

The Taming of the shrew (1967) Richard Burton, Elizabeth Taylor. Dir. Franco Zeffirelli. A sparking adaptation of Shakespeare's comedy, in which manly Richard Burton takes Elizabeth Taylor's bossy female down a peg or two.

The Velvet Touch (1948) Rosalind Russell, Leo Genn, Leon Ames, Sydney Greenstreet. Theatre actress Russell [Female Child] wants to escape the clutches of her Sugar-Daddy manager (Ames) after falling in love with suave, experienced Leo Genn. This film's first hour is better than the last 30 minutes but it has some great, sharp dialogue, well delivered by its stars. Leon Ames gives a good portrayal of a Sugar-Daddy losing his 'investment' and Leo Genn displays many of the 'cool' attributes of a Classical Man edging into Sugar-Daddy territory. IMDB rating 6.7

The Little Foxes (1941) Bette Davis, Herbert Marshall, Dan Duryea. Dir: William Wyler. Written by Lillian Hellman. Set in the Deep South at the turn of the 20th century this film focuses on the ruthless, rich Hubbard clan. Bette Davis does a fine turn as Matriarch [Female Parent] Regina Giddons née Hubbard manipulating, controlling and commanding all alike, male and female, to get her own way. How will the men cope? However, for the purposes of this book, the most interesting character is David Hewitt (Richard Carlson). It is this character who represents the Classical Man as the quietly effective male, who gently leads Regina's daughter Alexandria from Female Child to Female Adult.

FURTHER READING:

'How to be a Man and Attract Women - A Male Manifesto' (2013) Robert Laynton Companion Guides

There is a sense in which you are engaged in a confrontation, a battle, with the female in your life. Whilst she is not your *enemy* – she is sometimes your adversary. In this sense, the old adage remains true – 'Know your enemy'. To that effect, it is useful to know how females approach their relationships with males. You are half way there if you know their plans and tactics. With this in mind I recommend:

Powell, Ashley. 'Femme Fatale: How to trap the men of your dreams' Available on Kindle.

Fiction:

'Gone with the wind' (1988) Margaret Mitchell. Pan The book is even better than the classic movie, and it is not, as many suppose, a mere romantic story for females.

'Wuthering Heights' Emily Bronte (2010) Collins Classics

Self-help: Self confidence and assertiveness -

'Your erroneous zones. Escape negative thinking and take control of your life.' (2009) Wayne Dyer. Piatkus.

'Pulling your own strings' (1990) Wayne Dyer. Arrow

'Don't say 'Yes' when you want to say 'No''. (1998) Herbert Fensterheim & Jean Baer. Bantam

'When I say no I feel guilty. How to cope using skills of systematic assertive therapy' (1975) Manuel J. Smith. Bantam.

Gender differences:

'Men are from Mars, Women are from Venus' (2002) John Gray Thorsons

'Why men don't listen and women can't read maps' (2001) Alan and Barbara Pease. Orion

Transactional Analysis:

The concepts of Parent, Adult and Child are drawn from a psychology theory called Transactional Analysis. If you want to read more academic texts on this theme, then try:

'Transactional Analysis - 100 key points and techniques' (2009) Mark Widdowson Routledge

'T. A. Today. A new introduction to Transactional Analysis' (2012) Ian Stewart and Vann Joines Lifespace

Of related interest you can also try:

Rational Emotive/Behaviour Therapy:

'Reason to change. A Rational Emotive Behaviour Therapy workbook.' (2001) Windy Dryden. Routledge

Working with sub-personalities:

'Subpersonalities: The people inside us' (1989) John Rowan. Routledge

'Discover your subpersonalities: Our inner world and the people in it' (1993) John Rowan. Routledge

'What we may be: The vision and techniques of Psychosynthesis' (1990) Piero Ferrucci. Aquarius

ABOUT THIS BOOK

This book is an introductory version of the textbook 'Staying on top of your woman - A man's guide to dealing with the women in his life' by Robert Laynton and Thomas Katt Esq.. This introductory version keeps all the main elements of the original textbook – such as politically incorrect humor - but it is written in a lighter style and with lots of illustrations. It is aimed at any male – aged 15 to 50 – who is struggling a little in his relationship with his girlfriend, wife or female partner, and who would like a bit of help from his fellow male companions.

ABOUT THE AUTHOR

Inspired by Thomas Katt Esq., and with the help of numerous friends, both male and female, Robert Laynton collated many anecdotes, conversations and discussions bringing to them his Psychology and Counseling training in writing this book. He obtained an Honors degree in Psychology with the Open University and Post Graduate Certificate and Diploma qualifications in Counseling at Keele University in Staffordshire, England. He is now retired and continues to live in the U.K.